Department of Public Information

BASIC FACTS

about the United Nations

United Nations, New York, 1987

Note: Data effective 30 June 1987

ISBN: 92-1-100299-0

UNITED NATIONS PUBLICATION
Sales No. E.88.I.3

00300

Contents

Foreword by the Secretary-General v

Chapter I. The United Nations:
            Origin, purposes and principles, structure

Preamble to the Charter 1
Purposes and principles 2
Membership 3
Amendments to the Charter 3
Official languages 4
Structure of the Organization 4
    General Assembly (4); Security Council (7); Economic
    and Social Council (9); Trusteeship Council (11); Inter-
    national Court of Justice (11); Secretariat (13)
Budget of the United Nations 14

Chapter II. The United Nations at work
             for international peace and security

Promoting peaceful relations 16
Peace-making and peace-keeping 18
Afghanistan 19
Central America 21
Congo 24
Cyprus 25
    United Nations Peace-keeping Force in Cyprus (25)
Iran and Iraq 29
Kampuchea 31
Korea 33
Middle East 35
    United Nations Truce Supervision Organization (36);
    United Nations Emergency Force (36); United Nations
    Disengagement Observer Force (38); United Nations
    Interim Force in Lebanon (41); United Nations Relief
    and Works Agency for Palestine Refugees in the Near
    East (44)
South Asia subcontinent—India-Pakistan 45
    United Nations Military Observer Group in India and
    Pakistan (46)
Disarmament 48
Outer space 55
Law of the sea 58
Apartheid 62

Chapter III. The United Nations at work for economic and social development

New international economic order 71
International Development Strategy for the Third United
   Nations Development Decade 72
United Nations programmes for economic and social
   development 73
Technical co-operation for development 75
   United Nations Development Programme (77); United
   Nations Volunteers (78)
Trade and development 79
   United Nations Conference on Trade and
   Development (79)
Transnational corporations and the world
   economy 81
Science and technology for development 82
Natural resources and energy 83
Protection of the environment 85
   United Nations Environment Programme (85)
Human settlements 86
   United Nations Centre for Human Settlements
   (Habitat) (87)
World food problems 88
   World Food Council (88)
Population assistance 89
   United Nations Fund for Population Activities (90)
Assistance to children 90
   United Nations Children's Fund (91)
The role of women in development 92
Youth and development 94
Aging and the elderly 95
Disabled persons 96
Refugees 97
   Office of the United Nations High Commissioner for
   Refugees (97)
Disaster relief and special economic assistance 99
   Office of the United Nations Disaster Relief
   Co-ordinator (99); United Nations Sudano-Sahelian
   Office (100)
International control of narcotic drugs and psychotropic
   substances 101
Prevention of crime and treatment of offenders 103

Training and research 105
    United Nations Institute for Training and Research (105);
    United Nations Institute for Disarmament Research (106);
    United Nations University (106); United Nations Research
    Institute for Social Development (107); International
    Research and Training Institute for the Advancement of
    Women (107)

Chapter IV.   **The United Nations at work**
                for human rights

Universal Declaration of Human Rights 108
International Covenants on Human Rights 109
Elimination of racial discrimination 111
The fight against torture 112
Complaints of violations of human rights 113
Putting and end to violations 114
Women's rights 115
Other human rights questions 116

Chapter V.   **The United Nations at work**
              for decolonization

International Trusteeship System 119
Non-Self-Governing Territories 121
Declaration on the Granting of Independence to Colonial
    Countries and Peoples 123
Namibia 126

Chapter VI.   **The United Nations at work**
               for international law

Judicial settlement of disputes 132
    International Court of Justice (132)
Development and codification of international law 135
    International Law Commission (135)
International trade law 137
    United Nations Commission on International Trade
    Law (137)
Other legal questions 138

Chapter VII.   **Intergovernmental agencies related**
                to the United Nations

International Atomic Energy Agency 141
International Labour Organisation 142

Food and Agriculture Organization of the United Nations .. 144
United Nations Educational, Scientific and Cultural
    Organization 145
World Health Organization 146
World Bank 148
    International Bank for Reconstruction and Development
    (148); International Development Association (149); International Finance Corporation (150)
International Monetary Fund 151
International Civil Aviation Organization 152
Universal Postal Union 153
International Telecommunication Union 154
World Meteorological Organization 155
International Maritime Organization 157
World Intellectual Property Organization 158
International Fund for Agricultural Development 159
United Nations Industrial Development Organization 160
General Agreement on Tariffs and Trade 161

Appendices

List of abbreviations 166
Growth of United Nations Membership, 1945-1987 167
United Nations Member States 168
    Date of admission (168); Scale of assessments (168);
    Population (168)
United Nations Information Centres and Services 172
United Nations Special Observances 177
For further reading 178

Foreword

The establishment of the United Nations in 1945 marked a new beginning in the affairs of the global community. In agreeing to its Charter and instituting a working system of international co-operation, Governments resolved to put relations between nations on a footing altogether different from the one which had caused recurrent conflicts and untold suffering over centuries. They made a joint determination to eradicate the scourge of war, strengthen peace in conformity with justice and international law, respect the equal rights of nations large and small, promote social progress, protect human rights and use the United Nations as a centre for harmonizing their actions in the attainment of these common ends.

The years since then have been years of constant and fundamental change. They have witnessed a vast increase in both the membership and the concerns of the United Nations. Through it all, the world Organization has registered a solid list of accomplishments. Peace-keeping forces sent into the field have contained hostilities. Peoples formerly under colonial rule have attained independence and full sovereignty. Refugees have been provided shelter and relief. More than 60 legal instruments have been adopted to promote respect for human rights. International law has been expanded and codified. Diseases have been wiped from the face of the earth.

But the United Nations does not exist in a vacuum. If the Organization is to have the capacity to achieve its goals, it needs the support of the peoples of the world. That support, in turn, must be based on an understanding of its accomplishments and of the reasons why its potential has not yet been fully realized. The United Nations Charter begins with the words "We the Peoples of the United Nations"; ultimately, it is to the peoples of the world that the Organization must render its account.

It is for this broad public that this book is written, to serve as a guide to the structures and activities of the United Nations. *Basic Facts*, revised and updated regularly for the past 20 years, is also a handbook for schools, non-governmental organizations, legislators, journalists and others.

It is my hope that readers will find this latest edition a useful source of information on the work of the United Nations in an increasingly interdependent world.

Javier Pérez de Cuéllar
Secretary-General

v

CHAPTER I

The United Nations:
Origin, purposes and principles, structure

The name "United Nations" was devised by President Franklin D. Roosevelt and was first used in the "Declaration by United Nations" of 1 January 1942, during the Second World War, when representatives of 26 nations pledged their Governments to continue fighting together against the Axis Powers.

The United Nations Charter was drawn up by the representatives of 50 countries at the United Nations Conference on International Organization, which met at San Francisco from 25 April to 26 June 1945. Those delegates deliberated on the basis of proposals worked out by the representatives of China, the Soviet Union, the United Kingdom and the United States at Dumbarton Oaks in August-October 1944. The Charter was signed on 26 June 1945, by the representatives of the 50 countries; Poland, not represented at the Conference, signed it later and became one of the original 51 Member States.

The United Nations officially came into existence on 24 October 1945, when the Charter had been ratified by China, France, the Soviet Union, the United Kingdom and the United States and by a majority of other signatories; 24 October is celebrated each year as *United Nations Day.*

Preamble to the Charter

The Preamble to the Charter expresses the ideals and common aims of all the peoples whose Governments joined together to form the United Nations:

WE THE PEOPLES OF THE UNITED NATIONS
DETERMINED

to save succeeding generations from the scourge of war, which twice in our lifetime has brought untold sorrow to mankind, and to reaffirm faith in fundamental human rights, in the dignity and worth of the human person, in the equal rights of men and women and of nations large and small, and

to establish conditions under which justice and respect for the obligations arising from treaties and other sources of international law can be maintained, and

to promote social progress and better standards of life in larger freedom,

AND FOR THESE ENDS

to practice tolerance and live together in peace with one another as good neighbours, and

to unite our strength to maintain international peace and security, and

to ensure, by the acceptance of principles and the institution of methods, that armed force shall not be used, save in the common interest, and

to employ international machinery for the promotion of the economic and social advancement of all peoples,

HAVE RESOLVED TO COMBINE OUR EFFORTS TO ACCOMPLISH THESE AIMS

Accordingly, our respective Governments, through representatives assembled in the city of San Francisco, who have exhibited their full powers found to be in good and due form, have agreed to the present Charter of the United Nations and do hereby establish an international organization to be known as the United Nations.

Purposes and principles

The purposes of the United Nations, as set forth in the Charter, are:

◇ to maintain international peace and security;

◇ to develop friendly relations among nations;

◇ to co-operate internationally in solving international economic, social, cultural and humanitarian problems and in promoting respect for human rights and fundamental freedoms;

◇ to be a centre for harmonizing the actions of nations in attaining these common ends.

The United Nations acts in accordance with the following principles:

✧ It is based on the sovereign equality of all its Members.

✧ All Members are to fulfil in good faith their Charter obligations.

✧ They are to settle their international disputes by peaceful means and without endangering peace, security and justice.

✧ They are to refrain in their international relations from the threat or use of force against any other State.

✧ They are to give the United Nations every assistance in any action it takes in accordance with the Charter, and shall not assist States against which the United Nations is taking preventive or enforcement action.

✧ The United Nations shall ensure that States which are not Members act in accordance with these principles in so far as it is necessary for the maintenance of international peace and security.

✧ Nothing in the Charter is to authorize the United Nations to intervene in matters which are essentially within the domestic jurisdiction of any State.

Membership

Membership of the United Nations is open to all peace-loving nations which accept the obligations of the United Nations Charter and, in the judgement of the Organization, are able and willing to carry out these obligations. *(For list of Member States, see* Appendices.*)*

New Member States are admitted by the General Assembly on the recommendation of the Security Council. The Charter provides for the suspension or expulsion of a Member for violation of the principles of the Charter, but no such action has ever been taken since the establishment of the Organization.

Amendments to the Charter

The Charter can be amended by a vote of two thirds of the Members of the General Assembly and ratification by two thirds of the Members of the United Nations, including the five permanent members of the Security Council. So far, four Charter Articles have been amended, one of them twice:

✧ in 1965, the membership of the Security Council was increased from 11 to 15 (Article 23) and the number of affirmative votes needed on procedural matters was increased from seven to nine; on all other matters it was also increased to nine, including the concurring votes of the five permanent members (Article 27);

◆ in 1965, the membership of the Economic and Social Council was increased from 18 to 27 and, in 1973, was further increased to 54 (Article 61);

◆ in 1968, the number of votes required in the Security Council to convene a General Conference to review the Charter was increased from seven to nine (Article 109).

Official languages

Under the Charter the official languages of the United Nations are Chinese, English, French, Russian and Spanish. Arabic has been added as an official language of the General Assembly, the Security Council and the Economic and Social Council.

Structure of the Organization

The Charter established six principal organs of the United Nations:

GENERAL ASSEMBLY The General Assembly is the main deliberative organ. It is composed of representatives of all Member States, each of which has one vote. Decisions on important questions, such as recommendations on peace and security, admission of new Members and budgetary matters, require a two-thirds majority. Decisions on other questions are reached by a simple majority.

Functions and powers. Under the Charter, the functions and powers of the General Assembly include the following:

◆ to consider and make recommendations on the principles of co-operation in the maintenance of international peace and security, including the principles governing disarmament and the regulation of armaments;

◆ to discuss any question relating to international peace and security and, except where a dispute or situation is currently being discussed by the Security Council, to make recommendations on it;

◆ to discuss and, with the same exception, make recommendations on any question within the scope of the Charter or affecting the powers and functions of any organ of the United Nations;

✧ to initiate studies and make recommendations to promote international political co-operation, the development and codification of international law; the realization of human rights and fundamental freedoms for all, and international collaboration in economic, social, cultural, educational and health fields;

✧ to make recommendations for the peaceful settlement of any situation, regardless of origin, which might impair friendly relations among nations;

✧ to receive and consider reports from the Security Council and other United Nations organs;

✧ to consider and approve the United Nations budget and to apportion the contributions among Members;

✧ to elect the non-permanent members of the Security Council, the members of the Economic and Social Council and those members of the Trusteeship Council that are elected; to elect jointly with the Security Council the Judges of the International Court of Justice; and, on the recommendation of the Security Council, to appoint the Secretary-General.

Under the "Uniting for peace" resolution adopted by the General Assembly in November 1950, the Assembly may take action if the Security Council, because of a lack of unanimity of its permanent members, fails to act in a case where there appears to be a threat to the peace, breach of the peace or act of aggression. The Assembly is empowered to consider the matter immediately with a view to making recommendations to Members for collective measures, including, in the case of a breach of the peace or act of aggression, the use of armed force when necessary to maintain or restore international peace and security.

Sessions. The General Assembly's regular session begins each year on the third Tuesday in September and continues usually until mid-December. At the start of each regular session, the Assembly elects a new President, 21 Vice-Presidents and the Chairmen of the Assembly's seven Main Committees. To ensure equitable geographical representation, the presidency of the Assembly rotates each year among five groups of States: African, Asian, Eastern European, Latin American, and Western European and other States.

In addition to its regular sessions, the Assembly may meet in *special sessions* at the request of the Security Council, of a majority of Members of the United Nations, or of one Member if the majority of Members concurs. *Emergency special sessions* may be called within 24 hours of a request by the Security Council on the vote of any nine members of the Council, or by a majority of the United Nations Members, or by one Member if the majority of Members concurs.

At the beginning of each regular session, the Assembly holds a *general debate*, in which Member States express their views on a wide range of matters of international concern. Because of the great number of questions which the Assembly is called upon to consider (146 separate agenda items at the 1986 session of the Assembly, for example), the Assembly allocates most questions to its seven **Main Committees**:

> First Committee (disarmament and related international security matters)
> Special Political Committee
> Second Committee (economic and financial matters)
> Third Committee (social, humanitarian and cultural matters)
> Fourth Committee (decolonization matters)
> Fifth Committee (administrative and budgetary matters)
> Sixth Committee (legal matters).

There is also a **General Committee** composed of the President and 21 Vice-Presidents of the Assembly and the chairmen of the seven Main Committees, and a **Credentials Committee,** appointed by the President at each session.

Some questions are considered only in plenary meetings, rather than in one of the Main Committees, and all questions are voted on in plenary meetings, usually towards the end of the regular session, after the committees have completed their consideration of them and submitted draft resolutions to the plenary Assembly.

Voting in committees is by a simple majority. In plenary meetings, resolutions may be adopted by acclamation, without objection or without a vote, or the vote may be recorded or taken by roll call.

While the decisions of the Assembly have no legally binding force for Governments, they carry the weight of world opinion on major international issues, as well as the moral authority of the world community.

The work of the United Nations year-round derives largely from the decisions of the General Assembly—that is to say, the will of the majority of the Members as expressed in resolutions adopted by the Assembly. That work is carried out:

> ✧ by committees and other bodies established by the Assembly

to study and report on specific issues, such as disarmament, outer space, peace-keeping, decolonization, human rights and *apartheid;*

✧ in international conferences called for by the Assembly; and

✧ by the Secretariat of the United Nations—the Secretary-General and his staff of international civil servants.

SECURITY COUNCIL The Security Council has primary responsibility, under the Charter, for the maintenance of international peace and security. The Council has 15 members: five permanent members—China, France, the Soviet Union, the United Kingdom and the United States—10 elected by the General Assembly for two-year terms.

Each member of the Council has one vote. Decisions on procedural matters are made by an affirmative vote of at least nine of the 15 members. Decisions on substantive matters require nine votes including the concurring votes of all five permanent members. This is the rule of "great Power unanimity", often referred to as the "veto" power. All five permanent members have exercised the right of veto at one time or another. If a permanent member does not support a decision but does not wish to block it through a veto, it may abstain.

Under the Charter, all Members of the United Nations agree to accept and carry out the decisions of the Security Council. While other organs of the United Nations make recommendations to Governments, the Council alone has the power to take decisions which Member States are obligated under the Charter to carry out.

Functions and powers. Under the Charter, the functions and powers of the Security Council are:

✧ to maintain international peace and security in accordance with the principles and purposes of the United Nations;

✧ to investigate any dispute or situation which might lead to international friction;

✧ to recommend methods of adjusting such disputes or the terms of settlement;

✧ to formulate plans for the establishment of a system to regulate armaments;

✧ to determine the existence of a threat to the peace or act of aggression and to recommend what action should be taken;

✧ to call on Members to apply economic sanctions and other measures not involving the use of force in order to prevent or stop aggression;

✧ to take military action against an aggressor;

✧ to recommend the admission of new Members and the terms on which States may become parties to the Statute of the International Court of Justice;

✧ to exercise the Trusteeship functions of the United Nations in "strategic areas";

✧ to recommend to the General Assembly the appointment of the Secretary-General and, together with the Assembly, to elect the Judges of the International Court.

The Security Council is so organized as to be able to function continuously, and a representative of each of its members must be present at all times at United Nations Headquarters. The Council may meet elsewhere than at Headquarters if it considers this advisable; in 1972, it held a session in Addis Ababa, Ethiopia, and the following year, it met in Panama City, Panama.

When a complaint concerning a threat to peace is brought before it, the Council's first action is usually to recommend that the parties try to reach agreement by peaceful means. In some cases, the Council itself undertakes investigation and mediation. It may appoint special representatives or request the Secretary-General to do so or to use his good offices. In some cases, it may set forth principles for a peaceful settlement.

When a dispute leads to fighting, the Council's first concern is to bring it to an end as soon as possible. On many occasions since the United Nations was founded, the Council has issued cease-fire directives which have been instrumental in preventing wider hostilities in many parts of the world. It also sends United Nations peace-keeping forces to help reduce tensions in troubled areas, keep opposing forces apart and create conditions of calm in which peaceful settlements may be sought. The Council may decide on enforcement measures, economic sanctions (such as trade embargoes) or collective military action.

A Member State against which preventive or enforcement action has been taken by the Security Council may be suspended from the exercise of the rights and privileges of membership by the General Assembly upon the recommendation of the Security Council. A Member State which has persistently violated the principles contained in the Charter may be expelled from the United Nations by the Assembly on the Council's recommendation.

A State which is a Member of the United Nations but not of the Security Council may participate, without vote, in its discussions when the Council considers that that country's interests are specially affected. Both Members of the United Nations and non-members, if they are parties to a dispute being considered by the Council, are invited to take part, without vote, in the Council's discussions; the Council lays down the conditions for participation by a non-member State.

ECONOMIC AND SOCIAL COUNCIL. The Economic and Social Council was established by the Charter as the principal organ to co-ordinate the economic and social work of the United Nations and the specialized agencies and institutions—known as the "United Nations family" of organizations.

The Council has 54 members who serve for three years, 18 being elected each year for a three-year term to replace 18 members whose three-year term has expired.

Voting in the Economic and Social Council is by simple majority; each member has one vote.

Functions and powers. The functions and powers of the Economic and Social Council are:

✧ to serve as the central forum for the discussion of international economic and social issues of a global or inter-disciplinary nature and the formulation of policy recommendations on those issues addressed to Member States and to the United Nations system as a whole;

✧ to make or initiate studies and reports and make recommendations on international economic, social, cultural, educational, health and related matters;

✧ to promote respect for, and observance of, human rights and fundamental freedoms for all;

✧ to call international conferences and prepare draft conventions for submission to the General Assembly on matters falling within its competence;

✧ to negotiate agreements with the specialized agencies defining their relationship with the United Nations;

✧ to co-ordinate the activities of the specialized agencies by means of consultations with and recommendations to them and by means of recommendations to the General Assembly and the Members of the United Nations;

✧ to perform services, approved by the Assembly, for Members of the United Nations and, upon request, for the specialized agencies;

✧ to consult with non-governmental organizations concerned with matters with which the Council deals.

Sessions. The Economic and Social Council generally holds two month-long sessions each year, one in New York and the other at Geneva. The year-round work of the Council is carried out in its subsidiary bodies—commissions and committees—which meet at regular intervals and report back to the Council.

Subsidiary bodies. The subsidiary machinery of the Council includes:

✧ six **functional commissions**: Statistical Commission, Population Commission, Commission for Social Development, Commission on Human Rights, Commission on the Status of Women, Commission on Narcotic Drugs;

✧ five **regional commissions**: Economic Commission for Africa (headquartered in Addis Ababa, Ethiopia), Economic and Social Commission for Asia and the Pacific (Bangkok, Thailand), Economic Commission for Europe (Geneva, Switzerland), Economic Commission for Latin America and the Caribbean (Santiago, Chile) and Economic and Social Commission for Western Asia (Baghdad, Iraq);

✧ six **standing committees**: Committee for Programme and Coordination; Committee on Natural Resources, Committee on Non-Governmental Organizations and on Negotiations with Intergovernmental Agencies; Commission on Transnational Corporations, Commission on Human Settlements;

✧ a number of standing **expert bodies** on such subjects as crime prevention and control, development planning, international cooperation in tax matters, and transport of dangerous goods.

Relations with non-governmental organizations. Under the Charter, the Economic and Social Council may consult with non-governmental organizations which are concerned with matters within the Council's competence. The Council recognizes that these organizations should have the opportunity to express their views and that they often possess special experience or technical knowledge of value to the Council in its work.

Over 600 non-governmental organizations have consultative status with the Council. They are classified into three categories: **category I** organizations are those concerned with most of the Council's activities; **category II** organizations have special competence in specific fields of activity of the Council; and organizations on the **Roster** are those that can make an occasional contribution to the Council, its subsidiary organs or other United Nations bodies.

Non-governmental organizations which have been given consultative status may send observers to public meetings of the Council and its subsidiary bodies and may submit written statements relevant to the Council's work. They may also consult with the United Nations Secretariat on matters of mutual concern.

TRUSTEESHIP COUNCIL In setting up an **International Trusteeship System**, the Charter established the Trusteeship Council as one of the main organs of the United Nations and assigned to it the task of supervising the administration of Trust Territories placed under the Trusteeship System. Major goals of the System are to promote the advancement of the inhabitants of Trust Territories and their progressive development towards self-government or independence.

The aims of the Trusteeship System have been fulfilled to such an extent that only one of the original 11 Trusteeships remains—the Trust Territory of the Pacific Islands (administered by the United States). The others, mostly in Africa and the Pacific, have attained independence, either as separate States or by joining neighbouring independent countries *(see* Chapter V*)*.

The Trusteeship Council acts under the authority of the General Assembly or, in the case of a "strategic area", under the authority of the Security Council. Under the Charter, its total number of members is to be equally divided between those members which administer Trust Territories and those which do not, a parity which is not currently maintained. As the number of administering countries has decreased, so has the size of the Council, there are now only five members: the United States (administering State) and the other permanent members of the Security Council (China, France, the Soviet Union and the United Kingdom). Being a strategic area, the Trust Territory of the Pacific Islands falls within the responsibility of the Security Council.

Voting in the Trusteeship Council is by simple majority; each member has one vote.

The Council meets in annual sessions, usually in mid-year. It also holds special sessions when required.

Functions and powers. The Trusteeship Council is authorized to examine and discuss reports from the Administering Authority on the political, economic, social and educational advancement of the peoples of Trust Territories and, in consultation with the Administering Authority, to examine petitions from and undertake periodic and other special missions to Trust Territories.

INTERNATIONAL COURT OF JUSTICE The International Court of Justice is the principal judicial organ of the United Nations. Its Statute is an integral part of the United Nations Charter.

The Court is open to the parties to its Statute, which automatically includes all Members of the United Nations. A State which is not a Member of the United Nations may become a party to the Statute on conditions determined in each case by the General Assembly upon the recommendation of the Security Council.

All countries which are parties to the Statute of the Court can be parties to cases before it. Other States can refer cases to it under conditions laid down by the Security Council. In addition, the Security Council may recommend that a legal dispute be referred to the Court.

Both the General Assembly and the Security Council can ask the Court for an advisory opinion on any legal question; other organs of the United Nations and the specialized agencies, when authorized by the General Assembly, can ask for advisory opinions on legal questions within the scope of their activities.

Jurisdiction. The jurisdiction of the Court covers all questions which States refer to it, and all matters provided for in the United Nations Charter or in treaties or conventions in force. States may bind themselves in advance to accept the jurisdiction of the Court in special cases, either by signing a treaty or convention which provides for referral to the Court or by making a special declaration to that effect. Such declarations accepting compulsory jurisdiction may exclude certain classes of cases.

In accordance with Article 38 of its Statute, the Court, in deciding disputes submitted to it, applies:

◇ international conventions establishing rules recognized by the contesting States;

◇ international custom as evidence of a general practice accepted as law;

◇ the general principles of law recognized by nations; and

◇ judicial decisions and the teachings of the most highly qualified publicists of the various nations, as a subsidiary means for determining the rules of law.

Membership. The Court consists of 15 Judges elected by the General Assembly and the Security Council, voting independently. They are chosen on the basis of their qualifications, not on the basis of nationality, and care is taken to ensure that the principal legal systems of the world are represented in the Court. No two Judges can be nationals of the same State. The Judges serve for a term of nine years and may be re-elected. They cannot engage in any other occupation during their term of office.

The Court normally sits in plenary session, but it may also form smaller units called chambers if the parties so request. Judgements given by chambers are considered as rendered by the full Court.

The seat of the Court is at The Hague, Netherlands. *(See also* Chapter VI.*)*

SECRETARIAT The Secretariat services the other organs of the United Nations and administers the programmes and policies laid down by them. At its head is the Secretary-General, who is appointed by the General Assembly on the recommendation of the Security Council.

Secretary-General. The first Secretary-General of the United Nations was Trygve Lie, of Norway, who served until 1953. Dag Hammarskjöld, of Sweden, served from 1953 until his death in a plane crash in Africa in 1961. U Thant, of Burma, served until 1971. He was succeeded by Kurt Waldheim, of Austria, who held the office from 1972 to 1981. The present Secretary-General is Javier Pérez de Cuéllar, of Peru, who took office on 1 January 1982.

As one of his many functions, the Secretary-General may bring to the attention of the Security Council any matter which, in his opinion, threatens international peace and security, and may use his good offices to help in resolving international disputes.

The Secretariat, an international staff of more than 25,000 men and women from over 150 countries, carries out the day-to-day work of the United Nations both at Headquarters in New York and in offices and centres around the world. These international civil servants take an oath not to seek or receive instructions from any Government or outside authority.

Under Article 100 of the Charter, each Member State undertakes to respect the exclusively international character of the responsibilities of the Secretary-General and the staff and not to seek to influence them in the discharge of their duties.

The work of the Secretariat is as varied as the list of problems dealt with by the United Nations. It includes: administering peacekeeping operations; organizing international conferences on problems of world-wide concern; surveying world economic and social trends and problems; preparing studies on such subjects as human rights, disarmament and development; and interpreting speeches, translating documents and supplying the world's communications media with information about the United Nations.

Budget of the United Nations

The regular programme budget of the United Nations is approved by the General Assembly biennially. The budget is submitted initially by the Secretary-General and reviewed by a 16-member expert committee—the **Advisory Committee on Administrative and Budgetary Questions**. The programmatic aspects are reviewed by the 21-member **Committee for Programme and Co-ordination**.

For the 1986-1987 biennium, the budget appropriations, as revised in 1986, totalled $1,711,801,200, divided into 11 main categories of expenditures, as follows (in United States dollars):

I.	Over-all policy-making, direction and co-ordination	46,148,900
II.	Political and Security Council affairs, peace-keeping activities	94,625,400
III.	Political affairs, trusteeship and decolonization	30,677,700
IV.	Economic, social and humanitarian activities	477,410,900
V.	International justice and law	27,767,700
VI.	Public information	76,182,700
VII.	Common support services (administration and management; conference and library services)	649,546,400
VIII.	United Nations bond issue	16,758,600
IX.	Staff assessment	261,259,800
X.	Capital expenditures (construction, alteration, improvement and major maintenance of premises)	30,823,100
XI.	Special grants (grant to UNITAR)	600,000

Revised income estimates for the biennium 1986-1987, other than assessments on Member States, totalled $304,745,100:

I.	Income from staff assessment	265,126,700
II.	Other income (general income and revenue-producing activities)	39,618,400

The main source of funds for the regular budget are the contributions of Member States, who are assessed on a scale specified by the Assembly on the recommendation of the 18-member **Committee**

on Contributions. The fundamental criterion on which the scale of assessments is based is the real capacity to pay of Member States. The Assembly has fixed a maximum of 25 per cent of the budget for any one contributor and a minimum of 0.01 per cent. *(For scale of assessments of Member States, see* Appendices.*)*

The regular programme budget to which these assessments apply covers expenses relating to substantive programmes, programme support and administrative activities of the Organization both at Headquarters and around the globe. Outside the regular budget, Member States are also assessed, in accordance with a modified version of the basic scale, for the costs of the United Nations Interim Force in Lebanon and the United Nations Disengagement Observer Force in the Middle East.

Many other United Nations activities are financed mainly by voluntary contributions outside the regular budget. These programmes and funds include the United Nations Development Programme, the World Food Programme, the Office of the United Nations High Commissioner for Refugees, the United Nations Children's Fund, the United Nations Relief and Works Agency for Palestine Refugees in the Near East, and the United Nations Fund for Population Activities.

CHAPTER II

The United Nations at work for international peace and security

The United Nations Charter incorporates the solemn declaration that the peoples of the United Nations are determined to live together in peace and to unite their strength to maintain international peace and security.

Under the Charter, the Security Council is given primary responsibility for the maintenance of international peace and for the peaceful settlement of disputes. It has used such methods as mediation, good offices, stationing of military observers and peace-keeping forces *(these are discussed under* Peace-making and peace-keeping *below)*.

Promoting peaceful relations

The elaboration of principles or norms for the promotion of peace is carried out primarily by the General Assembly under Article 11 of the Charter, which states that: "The General Assembly may consider the general principles of co-operation in the maintenance of international peace and security. . . and may make recommendations with regard to such principles to the Members or to the Security Council or to both".

The main resolutions and declarations on peace, the peaceful settlement of disputes and international co-operation in strengthening peace adopted by the Assembly over the years include the following:

✧ the 1957 resolution on *Peaceful and neighbourly relations among States*, which stresses the need to develop friendly co-operation and peaceful relations among States irrespective of their divergencies;

✧ the 1965 *Declaration on the Inadmissibility of Intervention in the Domestic Affairs of States and the Protection of Their Independence and Sovereignty*, which condemns all forms of such intervention as contrary to the principles of the Charter and a threat to universal peace;

✧ the 1970 *Declaration on the Strengthening of International Security*, by which Member States are urged to make full use of the means and methods provided for in the Charter for the peaceful settlement of disputes and to agree on guidelines for more effective peace-keeping operations;

✧ the 1970 *Declaration on Principles of International Law concerning Friendly Relations and Co-operation among States in accordance with the Charter of the United Nations*, which sets forth seven principles, including the principle that States shall refrain from the threat or use of force against any State and the principle that States shall settle their international disputes by peaceful means;

✧ the 1974 *Definition of Aggression*, which calls upon States to refrain from all acts of aggression and recommends that the Security Council should be guided by the Definition in determining the existence of an act of aggression;

✧ the 1977 *Declaration on the Deepening and Consolidation of International Détente*, by which Member States declare their determination to strive to remove both causes and effects of international tension and to strengthen the role of the United Nations in maintaining international peace;

✧ the 1981 *Declaration on the Inadmissibility of Intervention and Interference in the Internal Affairs of States*, in which the Assembly recalled that the establishment, maintenance and strengthening of international peace and security are founded upon freedom, equality, self-determination, independence and respect for the sovereignty of States;

✧ the 1981 *Declaration on the Prevention of Nuclear Catastrophe*, which declares that any actions pushing the world towards a nuclear catastrophe are incompatible with human moral standards and the lofty ideals of the Charter;

✧ the 1982 *Manila Declaration on the Peaceful Settlement of International Disputes*, which recognizes the importance of enhancing the effectiveness of the United Nations in the peaceful settlement of disputes and in the maintenance of international peace and security.

Other actions of the General Assembly for the promotion of peace and of peaceful relations among States include the adoption:

✧ in 1978, of the *Declaration on the Preparation of Societies for Life in Peace*, in which the Assembly invited States to base their activities on the recognition of the need to establish, maintain and strengthen a just and durable peace, and called upon States to ensure that their policies are compatible with the goal of preparing entire societies, and, in particular, the young generations, for life in peace; and,

✧ in 1984, of the **Declaration on the Right of Peoples to Peace**, proclaiming that the world's peoples have a sacred right to peace, the preservation and promotion of which is a fundamental obligation of each State.

In March 1987, a special committee of the General Assembly completed for the Assembly's consideration the text of a draft Declaration on the Enhancement of the Effectiveness of the Principle of Refraining from the Threat or Use of Force in International Relations, under which no State was to use economic, political or other measures to coerce another State to subordinate its sovereign rights or secure advantages.

In 1980, the Assembly approved the establishment of the **University for Peace**, located in San José, Costa Rica.

The Assembly has designated the opening day of its regular annual session—the third Tuesday in September each year—as **International Day of Peace**, and also designated 1986 as **International Year of Peace**.

Peace-making and peace-keeping

Throughout its history, the United Nations has often been called upon to prevent a dangerous situation from escalating into war, to persuade opposing parties to use the conference table rather than resort to arms, and to help restore peace, or at least halt the fighting, when conflicts occur. Despite frustrations and setbacks, the Organization has steadily developed its capacity as a peace-making and peace-keeping organization.

The methods and machinery for preventing or terminating conflicts have taken many forms. In some disputes, the United Nations has acted through peace-keeping forces, observer or fact-finding missions (dispatched by the Security Council or General Assembly), plebiscite supervision, good offices missions, conciliation panels, mediators and special representatives. In other matters, it has provided the forum for debate and negotiation and a channel for quiet diplomacy.

Under Article 25 of the Charter, Member States "agree to accept and carry out the decisions of the Security Council" in accordance with the Charter. Recommendations of other United Nations bodies do not have the mandatory force of Security Council decisions but may influence situations through their weight as the expression of world opinion.

The Security Council has exercised its power to recommend measures of a military nature, as in Korea in the early 1950s. Often the Secretary-General has made his good offices available to the parties in disputes, either directly or through a special representative, as in the cases of Afghanistan and Kampuchea.

Conflict-control measures known as peace-keeping operations have been authorized by the Security Council (or, exceptionally, by the General Assembly), normally with the consent of the parties, in order to enable the United Nations to help bring about the cessation of hostilities, prevent their recurrence and normalize conditions. There have been two types of such operations: United Nations military observer missions and United Nations peace-keeping forces.

Military observer missions, as in Kashmir, are composed of unarmed officers made available to the United Nations, on the Secretary-General's request, by Member States. The mission's function is to observe and report to the Secretary-General (who in turn informs the Security Council) on the maintenance of a cease-fire, to investigate violations and to do what it can to improve the situation.

Peace-keeping forces are composed of contingents of armed troops made available by Member States. These forces typically assist in preventing the recurrence of fighting, in restoring and maintaining order and in promoting a return to normal conditions. To this end, peace-keeping forces are authorized as necessary to use negotiation, persuasion, observation and fact-finding. They run patrols or interpose themselves physically between the opposing parties. They must at all times maintain complete impartiality and avoid any action that might affect the claims or positions of the parties. While they are armed, they are permitted to use their weapons only in self-defence. United Nations peace-keeping forces have played a significant role in the Congo (now Zaire), Cyprus and the Middle East.

Afghanistan

On 3 January 1980, fifty-two Member States requested an urgent meeting of the Security Council to consider "the situation in Afghanistan and its implications for international peace and security". They stated that Soviet military intervention in Afghanistan, which had taken place late in 1979, had destabilized the area and threatened international peace and security.

Afghanistan, the USSR and other States objected to the Council's consideration of the question on the grounds that it amounted to intervention by the United Nations in Afghanistan's affairs.

Afghanistan said that it had requested Soviet aid, including military aid, in conformity with a 1978 bilateral treaty of friendship, good-neighbourliness and co-operation. The USSR said that, over the preceding two years, Afghanistan had repeatedly appealed for Soviet support in order to repel armed intervention from outside and that the Soviet Union's decision to send a limited military contingent to Afghanistan had been taken in response to that request and was based on provisions of mutual treaty obligations.

On 7 January, the Council considered a draft resolution which would have deplored the armed intervention in Afghanistan as a violation of a fundamental principle of the United Nations Charter—namely, preservation of the sovereignty, territorial integrity and political independence of every State—and would have called for the immediate and unconditional withdrawal of all foreign troops from Afghanistan. The draft resolution was not adopted because of the negative vote of one of the Council's permanent members. The Council then decided to call an emergency special session of the General Assembly to examine the question of Afghanistan.

The Assembly, meeting in emergency special session that same month, reaffirmed that respect for the sovereignty, territorial integrity and political independence of every State is a fundamental principle of the Charter. It strongly deplored "the recent armed intervention in Afghanistan, which is inconsistent with that principle", and called for the immediate, unconditional and total withdrawal of the foreign troops from Afghanistan "in order to enable its people to determine their own form of government and to choose their economic, political and social systems free from outside intervention, subversion, coercion or constraint of any kind whatsoever".

Numerous communications to the Secretary-General throughout the following years reflected the strained relations between Afghanistan and Pakistan; each side charging the other with violations of its airspace, bombings and other cross-border incidents.

Throughout, the Secretary-General and his personal representative, whom he appointed for this purpose in 1981, were involved in intensive efforts to promote a political solution through negotiations—through consultations during visits to Pakistan, Afghanistan and Iran, and through several rounds of discussions, i.e. "proximity talks" involving the Foreign Ministers of Pakistan and Afghanistan at Geneva. Inasmuch as the issues were interrelated, the diplomatic process was aimed at achieving a comprehensive settlement.

An understanding was reached that the political settlement was to consist of a set of four instruments that would include: (1) a bilateral agreement on non-interference and non-intervention, to constitute the main framework for future relations between Pakistan and Afghanistan; (2) a second bilateral agreement on the voluntary return of refugees; (3) a declaration on international guarantees on the settlement, to be given by the two designated guarantors—the USSR and the United States; and (4) an instrument setting out the interrelationships between the first three instruments and the solution of the question of the withdrawal of foreign troops, in accordance with an agreement to be concluded between Afghanistan and the USSR.

By June 1985, the first three instruments were virtually completed. A trip to the area for consultations in March 1986 by the personal representative made it possible to work out a set of understandings which had the effect of breaking an impasse that had stalled the process in December 1985. Another round of discussions commenced in May 1986 and resumed in July and August, focusing on the fourth draft instrument. The gap between the stated positions of the two interlocutors on the time-frame and modalities for the withdrawal of troops was the major question discussed at the next round in February/March 1987, following which the interlocutors returned to their capitals for consultations. The USSR and the United States had stated that they were ready to sign the guarantees as soon as an overall settlement acceptable to them was achieved.

The General Assembly has each year expressed appreciation for, and asked the Secretary-General to continue, his efforts, keeping Member States and the Security Council informed on progress. It has called upon all the parties concerned to work for the urgent achievement of a political solution and the creation of the necessary conditions which would enable Afghan refugees to return voluntarily to their homes in safety and honour. The Assembly has also appealed to all States and national and international organizations to extend humanitarian relief assistance to alleviate the hardships of the Afghan refugees, in co-ordination with the United Nations High Commissioner for Refugees.

Central America

In March 1982, Nicaragua asked the Security Council to meet in view of the "worsening of tension in Central America, with the ever-increasing danger of a large-scale military intervention by the armed forces of the United States". Denying the allegations as without foundation, the United States charged the Nicaraguan Government with large-scale intervention in the affairs of neighbouring countries and of aggressive conduct designed to destabilize neighbouring countries.

A draft resolution by which the Council would have appealed to all Member States to refrain from the direct, indirect, overt or covert use of force against any country of Central America and the Caribbean, and would have appealed to all parties concerned to use dialogue and negotiation, was not adopted owing to the negative vote of a permanent member of the Council.

Throughout the following years, in letters and statements to the Security Council, which met on several occasions at Nicaragua's request, Nicaragua and Honduras lodged accusations and counteraccusations of foreign interference, of numerous border incidents and of incursions by sea and by air. It was pointed out that military and naval manoeuvres, the presence of military advisers and forces from outside the region, the traffic in arms, the activities of armed groups, and the unprecedented buildup of arms and military and paramilitary forces constituted additional factors of tension. The situation was further aggravated by the growing number of refugees in the region, by severe economic recession which the Central American countries had been experiencing during the decade, and by a series of natural disasters, particularly earthquakes, which had befallen several of the countries.

Colombia, Mexico, Panama and Venezuela, which comprise the countries of the Contadora Group—so called after a meeting of their Foreign Ministers in January 1983 on an island off the coast of Panama—initiated a series of consultations with five Central American Governments (Costa Rica, El Salvador, Guatemala, Honduras and Nicaragua) in efforts to find a negotiated political solution to the problems affecting the region. In 1984, they elaborated a draft comprehensive agreement entitled the "Contadora Act on Peace and Cooperation in Central America", for signature and ratification by the five Central American States. Negotiations continued on unresolved aspects of the draft during the next year, with the backing of a Contadora Support Group created by the Governments of Argentina, Brazil, Peru and Uruguay in July 1985. A final version of the Act was delivered to the Secretary-General in July 1986.

The Security Council met again in May 1983 at the request of Nicaragua, which described what it termed the launching of a new stage of the invasion of Nicaragua "by counter-revolutionary Somozist forces operating out of Honduras and financed, trained and supported" by the United States. The Council unanimously adopted a resolution reaffirming the right of Nicaragua and of all the other Central American countries to live in peace and security, free from outside interference, commending and urging pursuit of the efforts of the Contadora Group, and asking the interested States to co-operate with it through a frank and constructive dialogue. The Council also asked the Secretary-General to keep it informed of developments in the area.

The Council met on several occasions in 1984, 1985 and 1986 to consider complaints by Nicaragua. In April 1985, at a meeting following the mining of a number of Nicaraguan ports, a Nicaraguan draft resolution addressing that topic was not adopted because of the negative vote of a permanent member. In May 1985, the Council unanimously reaffirmed Nicaragua's right freely to decide on its own political, economic and social systems without outside interference, called on the United States and Nicaragua to resume the dialogue they had been holding in Mexico towards normalizing their relations, and reaffirmed its support for the Contadora Group. The bilateral talks in Mexico, however, were not resumed.

The Council met in July and October 1986, at Nicaragua's request, on the dispute which had been the subject of a Judgment of the International Court of Justice of 27 June 1986 *(see section on Judicial settlement of disputes in Chapter VI)*. Draft resolutions which would have urgently called for full compliance with the Judgment were defeated due to the negative vote of a permanent member. A General Assembly resolution adopted in November 1986, however, contained such a provision.

The Assembly considered the situation in Central America during its 1983, 1984 and 1986 regular sessions. In 1983, it condemned acts of aggression against the States of the region. Especially serious in this context, it stated, were the attacks launched from outside Nicaragua against its strategic installations, the continued destruction and loss of life in El Salvador and Honduras, and the increase in the number of refugees in several of the region's countries. It has urged States to respect the purposes and principles of the draft Contadora Act and has continued to express support for the Contadora Group and its Support Group, asking them to persevere in their efforts.

The United Nations Secretary-General, together with the Secretary-General of the Organization of American States, extended in November 1986 a joint offer of services to the five Central American countries as well as to the eight Contadora and Support Group countries, bringing to their attention the resources available to the two organizations, with the aim of promoting or, where appropriate, complementing the Contadora peace initiatives.

The two Secretaries-General visited the five Central American countries in January 1987, at the invitation of the eight Ministers of the Contadora and Support Groups, with a view to resuming the peace initiative and reactivating the negotiating process.

Congo

The Republic of the Congo (Leopoldville) (now the Republic of Zaire), a former Belgian colony, became independent on 30 June 1960. In the days that followed, disorder broke out, and Belgium sent its troops to the Congo, stating that the aim was to protect and evacuate Europeans.

On 12 July 1960, the Congolese Government asked for United Nations military assistance to protect the national territory of the Congo against external aggression. Two days later, the Security Council called upon Belgium to withdraw its troops from the Congo and authorized the Secretary-General to provide the Congolese Government with such military assistance as might be necessary until, through the efforts of the Government with the technical assistance of the United Nations, the national security forces might be able, in the Government's opinion, to meet their tasks fully.

In less than 48 hours, contingents of a United Nations Force, provided by a number of countries including Asian and African States, began to arrive in the Congo. At the same time, United Nations civilian experts were rushed to the Congo to help ensure the continued operation of essential public services.

Over the next four years, the task of the **United Nations Operation in the Congo** was to help the Congolese Government restore and maintain the political independence and territorial integrity of the Congo; to help it maintain law and order throughout the country; and to put into effect a wide and long-term programme of training and technical assistance.

To meet the vast and complex task before it, the United Nations had to assemble an exceptionally large team. At its peak strength, the United Nations Force totalled nearly 20,000 officers and men. The instructions of the Security Council to this Force were strengthened early in 1961 after the assassination in Katanga province of former Prime Minister Patrice Lumumba. The Force was to protect the Congo from outside interference, particularly by evacuating foreign mercenaries and advisers from Katanga and preventing clashes and civil strife, by force if necessary as a last resort.

Following the reconvening of Parliament in August 1961 under United Nations auspices, the main problem was the attempted secession, led and financed by foreign elements, of the province of Katanga. In September and December 1961, and again in December 1962, the secessionist gendarmes under the command of foreign mercenaries clashed with the United Nations Force. Secretary-General Dag Hammarskjöld lost his life on 17 September 1961 in the crash of his aeroplane on the way to Ndola (in what is now Zambia) where talks were to be held for the cessation of hostilities.

In February 1963, after Katanga had been reintegrated into the national territory of the Congo, a phasing out of the Force was begun, aimed at its termination by the end of that year. At the request of the Congolese Government, however, the General Assembly authorized the stay of a reduced number of troops for a further six months. The Force was completely withdrawn by 30 June 1964.

Although the military phase of the United Nations Operation in the Congo had ended, civilian aid continued in the largest single programme of assistance undertaken until that time by the world Organization and its agencies, with some 2,000 experts at work in the nation at the peak of the programme in 1963-1964.

Cyprus

Cyprus became independent in 1960 with a Constitution that was intended to balance the interests of the island's Greek Cypriot and Turkish Cypriot communities. A treaty of August 1960, entered into by Cyprus, Greece, Turkey and the United Kingdom, guaranteed the basic provisions of the Constitution and the territorial integrity and sovereignty of Cyprus.

Following the outbreak of fighting in the island in December 1963, the Security Council met to consider a complaint by Cyprus charging intervention in its internal affairs and aggression by Turkey. Cyprus declared that the root of the problem lay in the divisive provisions of the Constitution, which had split the people into hostile camps. Turkey maintained that Greek Cypriot leaders had tried for more than two years to nullify the rights of the Turkish Cypriot community. It denied all charges of aggression.

On 4 March 1964, the Security Council unanimously recommended the establishment of the **United Nations Peace-keeping Force in Cyprus (UNFICYP)** with a mandate to prevent the recurrence of fighting, help maintain law and order, and promote a return to normal conditions. Since 1964, the Council has periodically extended UNFICYP's mandate, usually for periods of six months at a time.

A *coup d'état* in Cyprus on 15 July 1974 by Greek Cypriot and Greek elements favouring *enosis* (union with Greece) was followed by military intervention by Turkey, whose troops subsequently established Turkish Cypriot control over the northern part of Cyprus.

Following the outbreak of hostilities, the Security Council unanimously called for a cease-fire and laid the basis for negotiations between Greece, Turkey and the United Kingdom, which were held at Geneva until mid-August 1974, when they broke down. A further Turkish military operation extended the area under Turkish Cypriot control in the north. A cease-fire came into effect on 16 August 1974.

Four days later, the United Nations High Commissioner for Refugees was appointed by the Secretary-General as *Co-ordinator of United Nations Humanitarian Assistance for Cyprus*. More than 200,000 people required assistance as a result of the dislocation caused by the hostilities. The High Commissioner continues to aid displaced persons, and UNFICYP provides support in carrying out these humanitarian efforts.

Concurrently with the functioning of UNFICYP, the United Nations has been active in promoting a peaceful solution and an agreed settlement of the Cyprus problem. This task, first entrusted to a mediator, has since 1968 been carried out through the good offices of the Secretary-General. Within that framework, intercommunal talks between the representatives of the Greek Cypriot and Turkish Cypriot communities, as well as high-level meetings, have been held in an effort to reach a just and lasting solution to the problem.

In November 1974, the General Assembly unanimously called on all States to respect the sovereignty, territorial integrity, independence and non-alignment of Cyprus. It urged the speedy withdrawal of all foreign armed forces from Cyprus, a halt to foreign interference, and the safe return of all refugees to their homes. The Assembly said that constitutional issues were up to the Greek Cypriot and Turkish Cypriot communities to resolve, and it urged the continuation of the contacts which were taking place between representatives of the two communities with the help of the Secretary-General.

These contacts were broken off after an announcement by the Turkish Cypriot leadership in February 1975 that the Turkish Cypriot administration would be "organized on the basis of a secular and federated state". In March 1975, the Security Council expressed regret regarding this unilateral move and called for new efforts to assist the resumption of negotiations. It asked the Secretary-General to undertake a new mission of good offices and to convene the representatives of the two communities under his auspices.

The talks called for by the Council began in April 1975 at Vienna, and three further rounds were held that year. During the third round, agreement was reached that the Turkish Cypriots in the south of the island would be allowed to proceed north with UNFICYP assistance and that a number of Greek Cypriots would be transferred to the north in order to be reunited with their families. Greek Cypriots in the north would be free to go south or to stay. UNFICYP would have free and normal access to Greek Cypriot villages in the north.

After the fourth round of talks, in New York, the General Assembly, in November 1975, again demanded the withdrawal without further delay of all foreign armed forces from Cyprus and the cessation of all foreign interference in its affairs. A further round of talks was held in February 1976, but wide differences persisted.

In February 1977, President Makarios and Rauf Denktash, leader of the Turkish Cypriot community, met in Nicosia under the auspices of the Secretary-General and agreed on new guidelines for the representatives of their communities in the intercommunal talks. The two sides agreed, in particular, to seek an independent, non-aligned federal and bicommunal Republic of Cyprus.

On that basis, a new round of talks was held at Vienna and Nicosia, but were not continued after June 1977. A further initiative of the Secretary-General led to a meeting at Nicosia in May 1979 between President Spyros Kyprianou and Rauf Denktash, at which an agreed basis for resuming the talks was reached. The talks resumed at Nicosia in June 1979 but, encountering difficulties, were recessed on 22 June and did not reconvene until August 1980, all under the auspices of the Secretary-General or his Special Representative, who in the interim had held extensive consultations with the parties. Although the talks continued for some two years, no decisive progress was made.

A resolution on the question of Cyprus adopted by the General Assembly at a resumed session in May 1983 was strongly rejected by the Turkish Cypriot side, which subsequently decided not to attend the intercommunal talks on the grounds that the resolution undermined the basis for the negotiations.

On 15 November 1983, the Turkish Cypriot authorities proclaimed a "Turkish Republic of Northern Cyprus". The Security Council, by a resolution adopted three days later, considered the declaration legally invalid and called for its withdrawal. It asked the Secretary-

General to pursue his mission of good offices towards achieving a just and lasting settlement in Cyprus.

Following further efforts in early 1984 to pave the way for a high-level meeting and permit reopening of the dialogue, the Secretary-General, in a new initiative, met separately at Vienna in August 1984 with representatives of the two sides. In the light of their favourable reaction to his proposals, he invited the leaders of the two communities to meet with him separately in New York. Three rounds of "proximity talks" were held between September and December 1984. In December, the Secretary-General presented to each side documentation resulting from the working points agreed at Vienna in August and from the proximity talks. It contained elements for a comprehensive solution of the problem through the establishment of a Federal Republic of Cyprus. At a joint high-level meeting in New York in January 1985, the Turkish Cypriot side informed the Secretary-General that it accepted the documentation; the Greek Cypriot side stated that it could accept it only as a basis for negotiations.

The Secretary-General tried to overcome the differences that emerged at that time through the preparation of a consolidated draft statement. This document was accepted by the Greek Cypriot side in April 1986, but not by the Turkish Cypriot side. Lower-level talks with the parties followed at London, Geneva and Nicosia in late 1985 and early 1986.

On 29 March 1986, the Secretary-General presented to both sides a draft framework agreement which he said preserved all the points on which agreement had been reached over the past two years and suggested possible solutions to remaining divergencies. The following month, President Kyprianou advised the Secretary-General that, before the Greek Cypriot side could express its views on the draft framework agreement, it was necessary that there be agreement on the withdrawal of Turkish forces and settlers, effective international guarantees and the application of the "three freedoms" (of movement, settlement and the right to property). To this end, he requested the Secretary-General to convene an international conference or, if that proved impossible, a high-level meeting. Mr. Denktash informed the Secretary-General that the Turkish Cypriot side accepted the draft framework agreement and could not accept any procedure for proceeding other than that contained in the draft.

The Secretary-General reviewed the situation with the two leaders in September 1986. Two high-level members of his staff undertook a mission to Cyprus, Turkey and Greece in November to explore ways of moving forward; another mission was sent to Cyprus in February

1987 for the same reason. Although efforts have been made by the Secretary-General to resume the negotiating process, both sides have maintained their positions and the impasse remains.

In the mean time, UNFICYP continued to carry out its daily task of supervising the cease-fire and maintaining close surveillance over the buffer area between the cease-fire lines, as well as making efforts to discharge its functions with regard to the security and well-being of Greek Cypriots in the north.

On 29 May 1987, the Force had a strength of 2,328, made up of contingents from Australia, Austria, Canada, Denmark, Finland, Ireland, Sweden and the United Kingdom. Costs are met by those Governments and the Government of Cyprus, and by voluntary contributions. Contributions, however, have not been sufficient to meet the cost of the Force. In May 1987, the Secretary-General reported the accumulated deficit as more than $150 million, which, he said, placed an unfair share of the cost on troop-contributing countries. He hoped that the Security Council could agree that the United Nations share of those costs should be financed from assessed contributions.

Iran and Iraq

The conflict between Iran and Iraq has been of continuing concern to the United Nations since the outbreak of hostilities in September 1980. On 22 September 1980, the Secretary-General appealed to both countries for restraint and a negotiated solution, and offered his assistance. The Security Council, meeting later the same month, called on Iran and Iraq to cease hostilities and urged them to accept mediation or conciliation. In 1982, the General Assembly affirmed the need for an immediate cease-fire and withdrawal of forces to internationally recognized boundaries, called upon all other States to abstain from actions which could contribute to continuation of the conflict and asked the Secretary-General to continue his efforts towards a peaceful settlement.

Since the beginning of the conflict, the Security Council has supported the Secretary-General's efforts, and those of his Special Representative, towards resolving the situation, with a view to achieving a comprehensive, just and honourable settlement acceptable to both sides. In addition, in seven resolutions and numerous statements, it has variously called for a withdrawal of forces to internationally recognized boundaries, for the cessation of military operations against civilian targets, for respect for the right of free navigation and commerce in international waters, for refraining from endangering peace and security as well as marine life in the Gulf region, for an exchange of prisoners of war, and for the possible dispatch of United Nations observers to verify and supervise a cease-fire and withdrawal. It has strongly condemned the use of chemical weapons and all violations of international humanitarian law and called for strict observance of the 1925 Geneva Protocol against the use of poison gas and bacteriological weapons.

Iran has held the position that the Council's actions have not been impartial, and has disassociated itself from the Council's resolutions. Iraq has indicated that it would abide by the resolutions.

The Secretary-General on four occasions dispatched specialists to investigate charges of the use of chemical weapons: in March 1984 and February/March 1986, teams visited Iran; in March 1985, a medical specialist examined Iranian patients hospitalized in Europe; and in April/May 1987, teams visited both countries. In their reports they concluded that chemical weapons had been used against Iranian forces. The 1987 report stated that Iranian civilians and Iraqi forces had also been injured by chemical weapons.

Two United Nations teams were also set up to inspect allegations of violations of undertakings given by Iran and Iraq in June 1984 that deliberate military attacks on purely civilian population centres in either country would cease. Once in 1984 and twice in 1985, the teams investigated complaints and reported their findings.

In January 1985, the Secretary-General, with the agreement of the two Governments, dispatched a fact-finding mission to Iran and Iraq to inquire into an Iraqi charge that Iranian military authorities had fired on prisoners of war and also to report on other concerns that both countries had expressed regarding the situation of prisoners of war and civilian detainees. The finding of the mission indicated that the fundamental purposes for which the 1949 Geneva Convention relative to the Treatment of Prisoners of War was adopted were not being fulfilled.

In April 1985, the Secretary-General travelled to Teheran and Baghdad, where he discussed with the two Governments an eight-point plan he had presented to them the month before. The proposals were based on the premise that the Secretary-General's overriding responsibility under the Charter was to seek to end the conflict and that, until that goal was achieved, he also had the responsibility under international humanitarian rules to try to mitigate its effects, in areas such as attacks on civilian population centres, use of chemical weapons, treatment of prisoners of war and safety of navigation and civil aviation. The proposals envisaged that both parties would enter into sustained discussion in all these respects with the Secretary-General.

Iran's position was that the application of specific conventions and protocols could not be conditional upon a cease-fire. It indicated that it was prepared to accept a comprehensive cessation of hostilities provided that two conditions—condemnation of the aggressor and payment of reparations—were met. Iraq's position was that any specific measures to mitigate the effects of war—including mutual troop-withdrawal, prisoner exchange and reactivation of all ports—must be clearly linked to a comprehensive cease-fire within a timetable.

Despite continuing efforts, further movement on the plan's proposals did not materialize. In October 1986, Iraq informed the Secretary-General that it did not consider the plan to be a balanced and practical means for initiating the process towards a comprehensive settlement. The following month, Iran said it considered that the plan could serve as a suitable basis for future efforts. Both sides reiterated their positions of principle.

The Secretary-General has continued the search for new approaches, stating that he remains prepared to undertake any steps that, with the co-operation of both parties, would halt the loss of life and bring nearer the prospect of peace.

Kampuchea

Following the outbreak of hostilities in December 1978 between Democratic Kampuchea and Viet Nam, the situation in Kampuchea and related developments in South-East Asia were considered by the Security Council. In January 1979, the Council met at the request of Democratic Kampuchea, which charged Viet Nam with aggression. The Council considered a draft resolution that would have demanded strict adherence to the principle of non-interference in the internal affairs of States and would have called on all foreign forces to observe a cease-fire, end hostilities and withdraw from Democratic Kampuchea. The draft resolution, and a similar one considered again by the Council in March, was not adopted because of the negative vote of one of the Council's permanent members.

The question was considered by the General Assembly at its regular session later in 1979 at the request of five Asian States—Indonesia, Malaysia, the Philippines, Singapore and Thailand. The Assembly adopted a resolution by which it called for the withdrawal of all foreign forces from Kampuchea, appealed to all States to refrain from any interference in the internal affairs of Kampuchea and resolved that the people of Kampuchea should be enabled to choose democratically their own government, without outside interference, subversion or coercion. The Assembly also appealed to all States and national and international organizations to render humanitarian relief to the civilian population of Kampuchea.

The International Conference on Kampuchea (New York, July 1981), convened by a 1980 decision of the General Assembly, adopted the Declaration on Kampuchea, which reaffirmed the basic principles for a political settlement and set out the elements of such a settlement. The Conference also decided to establish an *ad hoc* committee to assist it in seeking a comprehensive political settlement of the Kampuchean question.

At its regular session later in 1981, the General Assembly endorsed the Declaration on Kampuchea and the establishment of the *Ad Hoc* Committee. It requested the Secretary-General to follow the situation closely and to exercise his good offices in order to contribute to a comprehensive political settlement. The Assembly also appealed for the continuation of relief assistance to Kampucheans still in need, especially those along the Thai-Kampuchean border and in holding centres in Thailand, and requested the Secretary-General to continue his efforts in co-ordinating humanitarian relief assistance and in monitoring its distribution. Similar resolutions were adopted by the General Assembly at subsequent sessions.

The *Ad Hoc* Committee has met regularly at United Nations Headquarters since October 1981 and has also dispatched missions to consult with interested Governments in South-East Asia and other regions.

Reporting annually to the General Assembly, the Secretary-General has stated that, in the exercise of his good offices, he has maintained close contact with the States most directly concerned and other interested parties and that his Special Representative has also held talks with Governments in the region. Following a visit to the region in 1985 to encourage progress towards a settlement of the problem, the Secretary-General identified, in a report to the Assembly, the main elements of a political settlement. These included: withdrawal of all foreign forces from Kampuchea; non-return to the universally condemned policies and practices of the recent past; promotion of national reconciliation; exercise by the Kampuchean people of the right to determine their own destiny; respect for the independence, territorial integrity and non-aligned status of Kampuchea; ensuring the security and sovereignty of all States in the region; international guarantees for the supervision of the implementation of the agreements reached; and establishment of a zone of peace, freedom and neutrality in South-East Asia. Since that time, the Secretary-General has continued to exercise his good offices, with a view to facilitating the realization of these elements and the attainment of a comprehensive political solution consistent with the basic purposes and principles of the United Nations Charter.

The Secretary-General's annual reports also provide information on the programme of humanitarian assistance to the Kampuchean people, in operation since 1980, funded by voluntary contributions from Member States, and consisting of three major components—namely, operations within Kampuchea, at the border and within Thailand. He reported in 1986 that, in spite of more than $1 billion in aid provided by the international community as well as by non-governmental organizations and bilaterally, and considerable efforts by the Kampuchean people themselves, food production and health and sanitary conditions continued to cause concern in Kampuchea. The *United Nations Border Relief Operation* (UNBRO) is responsible for over 260,000 Kampuchean civilians in the evacuation sites. Since 1984/1985, when the entire Khmer population at the border had to move into Thailand, UNBRO has endeavoured to ensure the civilian nature of the encampments, thus enabling it to consolidate relief operations and improve health, nutrition and social welfare. Of some 228,000 Kampuchean refugees received into camps in Thailand assisted by the Office of the United Nations High Commissioner for Refugees, some 215,000 have been resettled since 1975.

Korea

The question of Korea was first discussed in 1947 by the General Assembly, which sought unsuccessfully to bring about a unified Korean State through nation-wide free elections. In 1948, separate governments came into being in South Korea and in North Korea.

On 25 June 1950, both the United States and the *United Nations Commission on Korea,* which had been established by the General Assembly in 1948, informed the United Nations that the Republic of Korea had been attacked that morning by North Korean forces. The Security Council, meeting that same day, declared the armed attack to be a breach of the peace and called for a cease-fire and withdrawal of North Korean forces to the 38th parallel.

Two days later, as fighting continued, the Security Council recommended that Members of the United Nations furnish such assistance to the Republic of Korea as might be necessary to repel the armed attack and restore international peace and security in the area. The United States announced that it had ordered its air and sea forces to give cover and support to the troops of the South Korean Government and, later, that it had also authorized the use of ground forces.

On 7 July, the Security Council voted to ask all Member States providing military forces in accordance with the earlier resolutions to make them available to a unified command under the United States. This Command was authorized to fly the United Nations flag. Sixteen nations sent troops, and five others supplied medical units. The Republic of Korea also placed all its military forces under what became the *United Nations Command*.

The Soviet Union, which had been absent from the Security Council for six months, considered the Council's decisions illegal, as did the People's Republic of China, and in November 1950 a Chinese volunteer force entered the fighting on the side of North Korea.

Fighting continued in Korea until 27 July 1953, when an Armistice Agreement was signed. The following year, a political conference was held, as provided in the Armistice Agreement, but failed to find a solution to the Korean question.

The *United Nations Commission for the Unification and Rehabilitation of Korea*, which replaced the United Nations Commission on Korea in 1950, remained in the country until 1973 when it was dissolved by the General Assembly in a consensus decision noting with satisfaction that a joint communiqué issued by North and South Korea on 4 July 1972 provided for the following three principles on the reunification of Korea: the reunification should be achieved independently, without reliance upon outside force or its interference; it should be achieved by peaceful means; and national unity should be promoted.

In 1974, the General Assembly urged North and South Korea to continue their dialogue to expedite peaceful reunification. It also expressed the hope that the Security Council would in due course give consideration to the dissolution of the United Nations Command in conjunction with appropriate arrangements to maintain the Armistice Agreement, pending negotiations and conciliation between the two Korean Governments leading to a lasting peace between them.

In 1975, the United States informed the Security Council that it was prepared to terminate the United Nations Command on 1 January 1976, provided that agreement was reached on arrangements for maintaining the Armistice Agreement.

After debating the question again at its 1975 session, the General Assembly adopted two resolutions which expressed differing approaches to the problem. The first (adopted by 59 votes in favour to 51 against, with 29 abstentions) asked "all the parties directly concerned" to negotiate on arrangements to replace the Armistice Agreement "so that the United Nations Command may be dissolved concurrently with arrangements for maintaining the Armistice Agreement". The second resolution (adopted by 54 votes in favour to 43 against, with 42 abstentions), called for an end to "foreign interference" in Korea and called upon "the real parties to the Armistice Agreement" to replace it with a peace agreement "in the context of the dissolution of the United Nations Command, and the withdrawal of all the foreign troops stationed in South Korea under the flag of the United Nations".

Middle East

From its early days, the United Nations has been concerned with the problem of the Middle East. In response to hostilities which have broken out at various times in the course of four decades, it has established peace-keeping machinery and formulated principles for a peaceful settlement. It continues its efforts to find a just and lasting solution of the underlying political problems.

1947-1949 The Middle East problem had its origins in the issue of the future of Palestine, which was brought before the United Nations early in 1947. At the time, Palestine was a Territory administered by the United Kingdom under a Mandate from the League of Nations. It had a population of about 2 million, two thirds Arabs and one third Jews.

In November 1947, the General Assembly endorsed a plan, put before it by the *United Nations Special Committee on Palestine,* for the partition of the Territory, providing for the creation of an Arab and a Jewish State, with Jerusalem to be placed under international status. The plan was not accepted by the Palestinian Arabs or by the Arab States.

On 14 May 1948, the Assembly appointed a United Nations Mediator, Count Folke Bernadotte, to promote a peaceful adjustment of the situation in Palestine. On the same day, the United Kingdom relinquished its Mandate over Palestine and the State of Israel was proclaimed. On the following day, the Palestinian Arabs, assisted by Arab States, opened hostilities against the new State. The hostilities were halted through a truce called for by the Security Council and supervised by the United Nations Mediator, with the assistance of a group of military observers which came to be known as the **United Nations Truce Supervision Organization (UNTSO)**.

When Count Bernadotte was assassinated on 17 September 1948, Ralph J. Bunche was appointed Acting Mediator. Under his auspices, armistice agreements were signed in 1949 by Israel and four Arab countries—Egypt, Jordan, Lebanon and Syria. UNTSO assisted the parties to the agreements, through Mixed Armistice Commissions, in supervising the application and observance of the terms of the agreements.

1956 Following Egypt's nationalization of the Suez Canal Company in July 1956, Israel and, subsequently, France and the United Kingdom intervened militarily against Egypt. The General Assembly, meeting in emergency special session, called for a cease-fire and withdrawal of those forces from Egyptian territory, and authorized the establishment of the **United Nations Emergency Force (UNEF)**, the first United Nations peace-keeping force.

UNEF supervised the troop withdrawals and was then deployed on Egyptian territory, with Egypt's consent, to act as a buffer between Egyptian and Israeli forces. It patrolled the Egypt-Israel armistice demarcation line and the international frontier to the south of the Gaza Strip and brought relative quiet to the area. The Canal, blocked as a result of the hostilities, was cleared by the United Nations.

UNEF was withdrawn in May 1967, at the request of Egypt.

1967 Fighting again broke out on 5 June 1967 between Israel and Egypt, Jordan and Syria. The Security Council called for an immediate cease-fire. When hostilities ended six days later, Israel had occupied Sinai and the Gaza Strip, the West Bank of Jordan, including East Jerusalem, and part of the Syrian Golan Heights. The Secretary-General, acting on decisions of the Council, stationed UNTSO observers in the Golan and Suez Canal sectors to supervise the cease-fire. Meeting in emergency special session, the General Assembly, on 4 July, called on Israel not to take any steps to alter the status of Jerusalem.

On 22 November 1967, the Security Council unanimously adopted *resolution 242(1967)*, which defined principles for a just and lasting peace in the Middle East. The principles to be applied were:

✦ withdrawal of Israeli armed forces from territories occupied in the 1967 conflict; and

✦ termination of all claims or states of belligerency and respect for and acknowledgement of the sovereignty, territorial integrity and political independence of every State in the area and their right to live in peace within secure and recognized boundaries, free from threats or acts of force.

The resolution also affirmed the need to guarantee free navigation through international waterways in the area, settle the refugee problem justly and guarantee the territorial inviolability and political independence of every State in the area, through measures including the establishment of demilitarized zones.

The Council requested the Secretary-General to designate a special representative for the Middle East to help achieve a peaceful and accepted settlement in accordance with the provisions of resolution 242. Gunnar V. Jarring, of Sweden, who was appointed to that post, initiated talks with Egypt, Israel and Jordan in December 1967 (Syria did not accept resolution 242). The talks were continued intermittently until 1973, but despite Mr. Jarring's efforts no significant progress could be achieved because of the differences of the parties on the basic issues.

1973-1987 *(For developments relating to Lebanon during this period, see separate section below.)* Large-scale fighting broke out again on 6 October 1973, when Egyptian forces in the Suez Canal sector and Syrian forces on the Golan Heights attacked Israeli positions. The Security Council, in resolution 338(1973) of 22 October, called on the parties to cease fire and to start immediately thereafter the full implementation of resolution 242(1967). It also decided that, concurrently with the cease-fire, negotiations should start between the parties concerned, under appropriate auspices, to establish a just and durable peace in the Middle East. As fighting continued, the Council demanded an immediate and complete cease-fire and the return of the parties to the positions they had occupied on 22 October, and it decided to set up immediately under its authority a new **United Nations Emergency Force (UNEF II)**. The Force, established with a complement of up to 7,000 men for an initial period of six months, was stationed in the Egypt-Israel sector.

On 21 December 1973, a Peace Conference on the Middle East was convened at Geneva under United Nations auspices and the co-chairmanship of the Soviet Union and the United States, with Egypt, Israel and Jordan attending. Before adjourning the next day, the Conference decided to continue its work through a Military Working Group which would discuss the question of disengagement of forces.

Those discussions led to an agreement between Egypt and Israel on the disengagement of their forces. Signed on 18 January 1974, at a meeting of the Military Working Group chaired by the UNEF Commander, the agreement included provisions for a partial Israeli withdrawal from occupied territory in the Sinai, the establishment of a buffer zone controlled by UNEF and areas of limited forces and armaments on both sides of the zone. The disengagement was completed on 4 March 1974 with UNEF assistance.

Israel and Egypt signed a second disengagement agreement in September 1975, providing for further Israeli withdrawals. These were completed in February 1976, and a larger new buffer zone was set up under UNEF control.

UNEF's mandate was renewed periodically by the Security Council until July 1979, when it was not extended and therefore lapsed. UNTSO observers remain stationed in Egypt in accordance with existing decisions of the Council.

An agreement on disengagement of Israeli and Syrian forces was signed by both parties at a meeting of the Military Working Group on 31 May 1974. The agreement also provided for an area of separation and for zones of limited forces and armaments on both sides of the area, and called for the establishment of a United Nations observer force to supervise its implementation. The Security Council therefore decided to set up immediately under its authority the **United Nations Disengagement Observer Force (UNDOF)**, with an authorized strength of 1,250 men, for an initial six-month period. The disengagement process was completed in June 1974.

The Council has repeatedly extended the mandate of UNDOF, which, in May 1987, had a strength of 1,344, comprising contingents from Austria, Canada, Finland and Poland, as well as a number of UNTSO observers.

Meanwhile, the General Assembly had increasingly turned its attention to other aspects of the Middle East question. In 1968, it decided to establish a *Special Committee to Investigate Israeli Practices Affecting the Human Rights of the Population of the Occupied Territories*, which reports annually to the Assembly.

In 1974, it reaffirmed "the inalienable rights of the Palestinian people in Palestine" to unhindered self-determination, national independence and sovereignty, and recognized the Palestinian people as a principal party in the establishment of a just and durable peace in the Middle East. It also invited the Palestine Liberation Organization (PLO) to participate in the work of the Assembly and United Nations international conferences as an observer.

The following year, the Assembly established the *Committee on the Exercise of the Inalienable Rights of the Palestinian People* and asked it to recommend a programme for the implementation of those rights. The Committee recommended that a timetable be established by the Security Council for the complete withdrawal of Israeli forces from the areas occupied in 1967. The evacuated areas, with all properties and services intact, would be taken over by the United Nations, which, with the co-operation of the League of Arab States, would subsequently hand them over to the PLO as the representative of the Palestinian people. The Assembly has endorsed the Committee's recommendations at successive sessions since 1976, but the Security Council has not acted on them.

In 1977, the Assembly called for the annual observance of 29 November as the *International Day of Solidarity with the Palestinian People.*

A new element was introduced in the Middle East situation in November 1977 when President Anwar Sadat of Egypt visited Jerusalem. Subsequently, direct negotiations between Egypt and Israel under United States auspices led to the conclusion, in September 1978, of two agreements, known as the Camp David accords—one on a framework for peace in the Middle East and the other on a framework for the conclusion of a peace treaty between Egypt and Israel, which was signed on 26 March 1979.

The Council of the League of Arab States, meeting in Baghdad in November 1978, called on all countries to refrain from supporting the treaty. The Committee on the Exercise of the Inalienable Rights of the Palestinian People expressed the view that the accords did not take into account the inalienable rights of the Palestinian people and were negotiated without the participation of the PLO. The General Assembly condemned "all partial agreements and separate treaties" which violated the rights of the Palestinian people, and declared that the Camp David accords and other agreements had no validity in so far as they purported to determine the future of the Palestinian people and of the Palestinian territories occupied by Israel since 1967.

Under the peace treaty, Israeli forces withdrew, in three stages, from the entire occupied Sinai, over which Egyptian authorities then took control. The forces were completely withdrawn by 1982.

In 1983, The Assembly endorsed the Geneva Declaration on Palestine that had been adopted by acclamation by the International Conference on the Question of Palestine (Geneva, August/September 1983), which also adopted a Programme of Action for the Achievement of Palestinian Rights.

The Assembly, at successive sessions, has endorsed the call by the Geneva Conference for the convening of an International Peace

Conference on the Middle East under United Nations auspices and in conformity with guidelines set out in a 1983 resolution:

◇ the attainment by the Palestinian people of its inalienable legitimate rights, including the rights to return, to self-determination and to establish its own independent State in Palestine;

◇ the right of the PLO to participate on an equal footing with other parties in all efforts, deliberations and conferences on the Middle East;

◇ the need to put an end to Israel's occupation of the Arab territories, in accordance with the principle of the inadmissibility of the acquisition of territory by force and, consequently, the need to secure Israeli withdrawal from the territories occupied since 1967, including Jerusalem;

◇ the need to oppose any Israeli policies and practices in the occupied territories, including Jerusalem, particularly the establishment of settlements, that are contrary to international law and United Nations resolutions and that constitute major obstacles to the achievement of peace in the Middle East;

◇ the need to reaffirm as null and void all legislative and administrative measures and actions taken by Israel, the occupying Power, which have altered the status and character of Jerusalem, including the expropriation of land and property and the proclamation of Jerusalem as the capital of Israel; and

◇ the right of all States in the region to existence within secure and internationally recognized boundaries, with justice and security for all the people.

The Assembly invited all parties to the Arab-Israeli conflict, including the PLO, as well as the United States, the Soviet Union and other concerned States, to participate in the Peace Conference on an equal footing and with equal rights.

The Assembly has requested the Secretary-General, in consultation with the Security Council, to continue efforts towards convening such a Conference. In 1986, it endorsed a call for setting up a preparatory committee, within the framework of the Security Council and with the participation of the Council's permanent members, to take the necessary action to convene the Conference.

The Assembly has often reaffirmed its conviction that the question of Palestine is the core of the Middle East conflict and that peace in the region is indivisible and must be based on a comprehensive, just and lasting solution of the Middle East problem under the auspices of the United Nations. It has also reaffirmed the need for Israeli withdrawal from the territories occupied since 1967, including Jerusalem.

It has determined that Israel's decisions to impose its laws and administration on Jerusalem and on the occupied Golan Heights are null and void.

* * * *

LEBANON Tension along the Israel-Lebanon border increased in 1972. Israel, which stated that it was acting in reprisal for raids carried out on its territory by Palestinian commandos, attacked Palestinian camps in Lebanon. In April 1972, at the request of Lebanon and in accordance with a Security Council decision, a cease-fire observation operation was set up by UNTSO in the Israel-Lebanon sector.

Another United Nations peace-keeping force was set up in March 1978 after Israeli forces invaded southern Lebanon following a Palestinian commando raid into Israel. The Security Council called on Israel to cease immediately its military action against Lebanon's territorial integrity, and it established the **United Nations Interim Force in Lebanon (UNIFIL)** to confirm the withdrawal of Israeli forces, restore international peace and security and help the Lebanese Government re-establish its effective authority in the area.

The Council has continued to extend UNIFIL's mandate from its original six-month period. The Force had a strength, in July 1987, of 5,778 personnel from nine countries: Fiji, Finland, France, Ghana, Ireland, Italy, Nepal, Norway and Sweden.

When Israeli forces completed their withdrawal from Lebanon on 13 June 1978, they handed over their positions in the border area not to UNIFIL but to Lebanese *de facto* forces (Christian and associated militias) supported and supplied by them. The area remained tense, and there were frequent exchanges of fire between those *de facto* forces and the Israel Defence Forces (IDF), on the one hand, and armed elements (mainly of the Palestine Liberation Organization and the Lebanese National Movement) to the north of the UNIFIL area of deployment, on the other. In July 1981, a *de facto* cease-fire came into effect, and the area remained generally quiet until mid-1982.

On 6 June 1982, after two days of intense exchanges of fire in southern Lebanon and across the Lebanon-Israel border, Israeli forces moved into Lebanese territory in strength. UNIFIL positions were overrun or bypassed, and Israeli forces reached and surrounded Beirut.

Meeting throughout June, July and August, while hostilities continued, the Security Council urgently called for an immediate halt to all military activities within Lebanon and across the border, and demanded that Israel withdraw all its military forces forthwith and unconditionally to the internationally recognized boundaries of Lebanon. It called upon all the parties to the conflict to respect the rights of the civilian populations, to refrain from all acts of violence against those populations and to facilitate the distribution of aid by United Nations agencies and non-governmental organizations. The Council demanded that Israel lift immediately the blockade of Beirut and called for the restoration of the normal supply of water, electricity, food and medical provisions.

On 1 August, the Security Council authorized the Secretary-General to deploy United Nations military observers to monitor the situation in and around Beirut. The United Nations observers assigned to the Israel-Lebanon Mixed Armistice Commission were constituted as the **Observer Group Beirut (OGB)**. A cease-fire went into effect on 12 August.

Later that month, France, Italy and the United States entered into an agreement with Lebanon for participation of their troops in a multinational force to assist Lebanese armed forces in carrying out an orderly departure from Lebanon of Palestinian armed personnel in the Beirut area.

The evacuation of the Palestinian armed elements and the Arab Deterrent Force from the Beirut area was completed on 1 September. The last elements of the multinational force were withdrawn on 13 September. However, tension greatly increased on 14 September when President-elect Bashir Gemayel and several others were killed in a bomb explosion. The following day, units of the IDF took new positions in the area.

The Security Council condemned the Israeli incursions into Beirut in violation of the cease-fire agreements and Council resolutions; demanded that Israel return immediately to its pre-15 September positions; and called again for the strict respect for Lebanon's sovereignty, territorial integrity, unity and political independence under the sole and exclusive authority of the Lebanese Government throughout Lebanon.

On the evening of 16 September, Kataeb (Phalange) units entered the Sabra and Shatila Palestinian refugee camps in the suburbs of Beirut. On 18 September, OGB observers reported finding many bodies of men, women and children in civilian clothes who had been massacred. The Security Council condemned the massacre, as did the General Assembly, which called for respect for and application of the (fourth) Geneva Convention relative to the Protection of Civilian Persons in Time of War, of 1949. In the wake of the massacre, the President of the United States informed the Secretary-General on 24 September that he was sending 1,200 troops back to Beirut, at the request of the Lebanese Government. French, Italian and United States contingents of the multinational force started returning to Beirut that day, later joined by a small British contingent.

The withdrawal of the IDF from the Beirut area began in late July 1983. This set the stage for fighting between Lebanese Government forces and Christian phalangists on the one hand, and Shi'ite and Druse militias on the other, in the evacuated areas. As hostilities intensified, French and United States contingents of the multinational force became embroiled in the fighting.

The situation in the Beirut area remained unstable, with continuing loss of life and destruction of property, throughout the remainder of 1983 and 1984. In view of the planned withdrawal of the four-nation multinational force from the area, the Security Council, in March 1984, considered a proposal introduced by France for deployment of a United Nations force in the Beirut area, after the withdrawal of the multinational force, to monitor compliance with the cease-fire and to help protect civilians, but it was not adopted.

In 1984, the Secretary-General convoked at UNIFIL headquarters a conference of military representatives of Lebanon and Israel, which met intermittently between November 1984 and January 1985, to expedite the orderly withdrawal of Israeli forces and to discuss related security arrangements.

On 22 January 1985, Israel presented to the conference a three-phase plan for unilateral redeployment and withdrawal of its forces, commencing in February, to be completed by mid-1985. During the third phase, the IDF would deploy along the Israel-Lebanon international border, while maintaining a "security zone" in southern Lebanon where "local forces" (the so-called South Lebanon Army (SLA)) would function with IDF backing. The Lebanese Government said it would not assign a role to any military force which was not a legal force, or accept buffer or security zones. The conference adjourned *sine die*.

During and after the withdrawal, both the number and intensity of attacks by Lebanese resistance groups against Israeli forces and Lebanese irregulars armed and controlled by them increased sharply. In part of its area of deployment, UNIFIL was confronted with many positions which overlapped those manned by IDF and/or local Lebanese forces, mainly the SLA, in the security zone. Attacks by Lebanese groups gave rise to countermeasures by Israeli and associated local forces and led to frequent and dangerous confrontations between those forces and UNIFIL personnel.

The Secretary-General has continued his efforts to persuade Israel to abandon the security zone, but has been unsuccessful. Israel, while reaffirming that it has no territorial designs in Lebanon, has argued that the Lebanese Government does not exercise effective authority in the area and that UNIFIL, being a peace-keeping force, is not mandated to take the forceful action necessary to control cross-border attacks. Lebanese authorities continue to insist that Israel withdraw its forces completely, stating that its occupation is illegal and contrary to United Nations resolutions and further escalates tension and conflict.

* * * *

UNITED NATIONS RELIEF AND WORKS AGENCY FOR PALESTINE REFUGEES IN THE NEAR EAST (UNRWA)

The United Nations Relief and Works Agency for Palestine Refugees in the Near East was established by the General Assembly in 1949 to help the refugees who lost their homes and livelihood as a result of the Arab-Israeli conflict in Palestine in 1948, pending the solution to their problem. According to an earlier Assembly decision, this was to be by means of repatriation or compensation.

UNRWA provides education and training, health and relief services to Arab refugees from Palestine in Jordan, Lebanon, the Syrian Arab Republic and the occupied territories of the West Bank and Gaza Strip. Its mandate has been renewed periodically by the General Assembly, most recently until 30 June 1990.

In the 1986/87 school year, UNRWA educated some 350,000 pupils in the elementary and preparatory cycles of education in 635 schools. Each year the Agency trains between 4,500 and 5,000 young people in vocational/technical and teacher training, and sends about 350 students to universities on scholarships.

In mid-1987, more than 2.2 million refugees were registered with UNRWA. UNRWA's health services have made a great difference in the health of the Palestine refugee population. Its medical services stress preventive medicine, mother and child health care, environmental sanitation and health education. Services provided at health centres and health points include specialized clinics for chronic and degenerative diseases and dental clinics.

Relief services comprise a "special hardship case" programme and a general welfare programme. The former concentrates on providing food and other welfare assistance to destitute refugees (about 5 per cent of the refugee population). The general welfare programme includes case work, emergency aid, training of adults and the disabled, pre-school and women's activities, and promotion of income-generating projects.

Since the Israeli invasion of Lebanon in early June 1982, UNRWA has mounted a series of emergency operations in that country to cope with its effects and with the further death, destruction and dislocation to Palestine refugees cause by continued interfactional and intra-Palestinian conflict there. A $60.3 million emergency relief programme, including food aid, in the aftermath of the invasion was phased out in 1984, having benefited some 178,000 Palestine refugees. Fighting in southern Lebanon and in Beirut in April/May 1985 required a further emergency operation for more than 26,000. Fighting in Tripoli in the fall of that year and in Beirut in mid-May 1986 led to other emergency operations. A seige by local militias of Rashidieh Camp in the Tyre area and Burj el Barajneh and Shatila Camps in Beirut in October/November 1986 required yet another emergency operation, which was still under way in mid-1987.

In all these operations, and particularly in the last one, UNRWA's activities were greatly hampered by kidnapping and killing of UNRWA staff and by the hijacking of trucks carrying relief supplies. Talks with the Lebanese authorities, Syrian military authorities and militia groups had not, by mid-1987, resolved these difficulties.

In his 1986 annual report, the Commissioner-General of UNRWA drew attention to the plight of refugees in Gaza, stressing population density (nearly 1,400 people per square kilometre), a shortage of adequate housing, rising unemployment, and increasing salinity of water supplies.

UNRWA depends on voluntary contributions, mainly from Governments, for both its normal and emergency operations.

South Asia subcontinent—India-Pakistan

For nearly four decades, the United Nations has been concerned with the dispute between India and Pakistan over Kashmir. In addition, the Organization mounted the largest humanitarian operation in its history during and after the conflict over Bangladesh in 1971.

The State of Jammu and Kashmir was an Indian princely State which became free, under the partition plan and the Indian Independence Act of 1947, to accede to India or to Pakistan, on both of which it borders. The Maharajah of the State requested accession to India and India accepted on the understanding that the question would be settled by reference to the people.

In January 1948, India complained to the Security Council that tribesmen and others, with Pakistan's support and participation, were invading Kashmir and that extensive fighting was taking place. Pakistan denied the charges and declared that Kashmir's accession to India was illegal.

The Security Council established a *United Nations Commission for India and Pakistan* to investigate and mediate, first on the Jammu and Kashmir situation and, when so directed by the Council, on other situations complained of by Pakistan. The Council also recommended various measures, including the use of observers, to stop the fighting and to create proper conditions for a free and impartial plebiscite. To assist in carrying out these measures, it instructed the Commission to proceed at once to the Indian subcontinent and there place its good offices and mediation at the disposal of the Governments of India and Pakistan.

The Commission made proposals to both India and Pakistan regarding a cease-fire and troop withdrawals and also proposed to the Governments that the accession of Jammu and Kashmir be decided by a free and impartial plebiscite. Both sides accepted the proposals, with clarifications and understandings. The cease-fire came into effect on 1 January 1949, and United Nations military observers were deployed in the area to supervise it. In July 1949, a cease-fire line was established in Jammu and Kashmir under an agreement between the two countries reached in Karachi under the auspices of the United Nations Commission.

India and Pakistan also accepted the proposal for a plebiscite, but the Commission was unable to reach agreement with the parties on the terms of demilitarization of the State before a plebiscite could be held. Despite mediation by various United Nations representatives, differences between the parties remained and the problem came before the Security Council at various times between 1957 and 1964.

Hostilities again broke out between India and Pakistan in early August 1965. The Security Council called for a cease-fire, and the fighting was brought to a stop in September 1965, with the assistance of the **United Nations Military Observer Group in India and Pakistan (UNMOGIP)**, which had been set up under the Council's 1948 resolution establishing the United Nations Commission for India and Pakistan. At the same time, the Secretary-General reported that he had decided to organize the observers who would supervise the cease-fire along the India-Pakistan border as the **United Nations India-Pakistan Observation Mission (UNIPOM)**, an operation distinct from UNMOGIP in Kashmir.

At a series of joint meetings of representatives of India and Pakistan, which had been convened by the representative of the Secretary-General in January 1966, a plan and ground rules for withdrawals were worked out. The Secretary-General reported that, on 10 January, the Prime Minister of India and the President of Pakistan had agreed, in a joint Declaration at Tashkent—where they met under the auspices of the Soviet Union—that their respective armed personnel would be withdrawn no later than 25 February to positions held before 5 August 1965. The withdrawal of troops was carried out in February 1966 under the supervision of UNMOGIP and UNIPOM military observers.

In 1971, another conflict broke out between India and Pakistan, this time in connection with civil strife in East Pakistan, which later became the independent State of Bangladesh. As millions of refugees streamed into neighbouring India, tension increased in the region. With the consent of India and Pakistan, the Secretary-General set up two large-scale humanitarian programmes—one, under the United Nations High Commissioner for Refugees, for the relief of East Pakistan refugees in India, and the other, under a United Nations representative, for assistance to the distressed population in East Pakistan.

In October 1971, the Secretary-General offered his good offices to the Governments of India and Pakistan in dealing with the deteriorating situation in the area, but this was not accepted by India. In December, when full-scale hostilities broke out between the two countries, he notified the Security Council, under Article 99 of the Charter, that the situation constituted a threat to international peace and security.

After a cease-fire had put an end to the fighting on 17 December, the Security Council demanded strict observance of it until withdrawals of all armed forces to their respective territories and to positions which fully respected the cease-fire line in Kashmir supervised by UNMOGIP. The Council also called for international assistance to relieve the suffering, and it authorized the Secretary-General to appoint a Special Representative to aid in the solution of humanitarian problems.

In July 1972, the Prime Minister of India and the President of Pakistan signed, at Simla, an agreement defining a Line of Control in Kashmir which, with minor deviations, followed the same course as the cease-fire line established in the Karachi agreement of 1949. UNMOGIP observers continue to be deployed along both sides of the line, but their activities have been restricted on the Indian side of the line.

During 1972, the refugees, with the assistance of the United Nations, returned to their homeland. The United Nations relief operation helped to pave the way for rehabilitation of the war-shattered economy of Bangladesh, which became a Member of the United Nations in 1974.

Disarmament

The Charter confers specific responsibilities in the matter of disarmament on the General Assembly and the Security Council. The Assembly is empowered to consider "principles governing disarmament and the regulation of armaments" and to make "recommendations with regard to such principles to the Members or to the Security Council or to both". The Council, "in order to promote the establishment and maintenance of international peace and security with the least diversion for armaments of the world's human and economic resources", is responsible for formulating, with the assistance of the *Military Staff Committee*, "plans to be submitted to the Members of the United Nations for the establishment of a system for the regulation of armaments".

The original bodies of the United Nations in the field of disarmament were the Atomic Energy Commission and the Commission for Conventional Armaments, which were set up by the Security Council in 1946 and 1947, respectively. They called for immediate plans to ensure that atomic energy would be used only for peaceful purposes and that armaments and armed forces would be generally regulated and reduced under an international system of control and inspection.

Despite the urgency of the matter, the two commissions did not make much progress. In 1952, the General Assembly, in an attempt to break the impasse, consolidated the two commissions into a single Disarmament Commission with the task of preparing proposals for the regulation, limitation and balanced reduction of all armed forces and all armaments in a co-ordinated, comprehensive programme by stages.

In recognition, however, of the need to pursue more far-reaching objectives, beginning in 1959 an item entitled "General and complete disarmament" was placed on the General Assembly's agenda. It represented the ultimate goal of all arms regulation and disarmament efforts.

Concerted efforts by the United Nations and by Governments have produced limited but important first steps in the form of international arms control agreements dealing particularly with the threat of nuclear weapons. Prominent among these are:

✧ the 1959 *Antarctic Treaty*, the first treaty to put into practice the concept of the nuclear-weapon-free zone, later applied to the sea-bed, outer space and Latin America; it prohibits in the Antarctic region any military manœuvres, weapon tests, building of installations or the disposal of radioactive wastes produced by military activities;

✧ the 1963 *Treaty Banning Nuclear Weapons Tests in the Atmosphere, in Outer Space and Under Water*, called the Partial Test-Ban Treaty because it does not ban underground tests; the General Assembly has repeatedly urged conclusion of a comprehensive treaty banning all tests, whether in the atmosphere, underground or under water;

✧ the 1966 *Treaty on Principles Governing the Activities of States in the Exploration and Use of Outer Space, including the Moon and Other Celestial Bodies* (Outer Space Treaty) bans nuclear and other weapons of mass destruction from the earth's orbit, prohibits the military use of celestial bodies or the placing of nuclear weapons on those bodies and bars the stationing of weapons in outer space, but does not prevent nuclear-weapon missiles or weapons satellites from moving through outer space, the use of space-based platforms for launching ballistic missiles or the use of satellites to control and operate nuclear weapons;

✧ the 1967 *Treaty for the Prohibition of Nuclear Weapons in Latin America* (Treaty of Tlatelolco) created the first nuclear-weapon-free zone in a densely populated area and is the first arms control agreement whose implementation is verified by an international organization;

✧ the 1968 *Treaty on the Non-Proliferation of Nuclear Weapons* (Non-Proliferation Treaty) aims at limiting the spread of nuclear weapons from nuclear to non-nuclear countries, at promoting the process of disarmament by the nuclear nations and at guaranteeing all countries access to nuclear technology for peaceful purposes;

✧ the 1970 *Treaty on the Prohibition of the Emplacement of Nuclear Weapons and Other Weapons of Mass Destruction on the Sea-Bed and the Ocean Floor and in the Subsoil Thereof* (Sea-Bed Treaty) bans the placement of nuclear and other weapons of mass destruction, and facilities for such weapons, on or under the sea-bed, outside a 12-mile coastal zone around each country, but does not mention conventional weapons or restrict the military use of the oceans;

✧ the 1971 *Convention on the Prohibition of the Development, Production and Stockpiling of Bacteriological (Biological) and Toxin Weapons and on Their Destruction* was the first international agreement providing for genuine disarmament—that is, the destruction of existing weapons;

✧ the 1976 *Convention on the Prohibition of Military or Any Other Hostile Use of Environmental Modification Techniques* prohibits the use of techniques that would have widespread, long-lasting or severe effects by causing such phenomena as earthquakes, tidal waves and changes in weather and climate patterns;

✧ the 1980 *Convention on Prohibitions or Restrictions on the Use of Certain Conventional Weapons Which May Be Deemed to Be Excessively Injurious or to Have Indiscriminate Effects* restricts or prohibits the use of mines and booby traps, incendiary weapons, and fragments not detectable by X-ray in the human body.

Despite these important agreements for limitation and regulation of armaments, global expenditures on arms and armies have continued to mount, and are currently estimated at over $900 billion per year, consuming material and human resources that might otherwise be applied to development purposes.

Recognizing the pressing need to slow and reverse the world-wide arms race, the General Assembly in 1969 proclaimed the 1970s as a *Disarmament Decade*. Governments were urged to intensify their concerted efforts for effective measures relating to the cessation of the nuclear arms race, to nuclear disarmament and to the elimination of other weapons of mass destruction.

By 1976, the Assembly, deploring the "meagre achievements" of the Decade in terms of truly effective disarmament and arms limitation agreements, decided to hold a special session in 1978 devoted entirely to disarmament.

The *first special session on disarmament*, held at United Nations Headquarters from 23 May to 1 July 1978, was the largest, most representative meeting of nations ever convened to consider the question of disarmament. For the first time in the history of disarmament negotiations, the international community of States achieved consensus agreement on a comprehensive disarmament strategy, which was embodied in the Final Document adopted at the session.

The 129-paragraph Final Document stresses the central role and primary responsibility of the United Nations in the field of disarmament and contains specific measures intended to strengthen the machinery that deals with disarmament issues within the United

Nations system. Its four sections also set out goals, principles and priorities in the field of disarmament:

❖ The *Introduction* states that while the final objective of the efforts of all States should continue to be general and complete disarmament under effective international control, the immediate goal is the elimination of the danger of a nuclear war and the implementation of measures to halt and reverse the arms race.

❖ The *Declaration* states that "the increase in weapons, especially nuclear weapons, far from helping to strengthen international security, on the contrary weakens it" and "heightens the sense of insecurity among all States, including the non-nuclear-weapon States, and increases the threat of nuclear war". Genuine and lasting peace "can only be created through the effective implementation of the security system provided for in the Charter of the United Nations and the speedy and substantial reduction of arms and armed forces. . . leading ultimately to general and complete disarmament under effective international control". In the adoption of disarmament measures, the right of each State to security should be kept in mind and at each stage of the disarmament process "the objective should be undiminished security at the lowest possible level of armaments and military forces".

❖ The *Programme of Action* lists priorities and measures that States should undertake as a matter of urgency in the field of disarmament. Priorities include: nuclear weapons; other weapons of mass destruction, including chemical weapons; and conventional weapons, including any which may be deemed to be excessively injurious or to have indiscriminate effects.

The Programme calls for agreements or other measures to be "resolutely pursued on a bilateral, regional and multilateral basis", and recommends that measures be taken and policies pursued to strengthen international peace and security and build confidence among States.

The urgency of preventing the proliferation of nuclear weapons and of halting nuclear tests is stressed. The Programme calls for full implementation of the 1967 Treaty of Tlatelolco, empowers the Security Council to take the necessary steps to avoid any setbacks to the proposed denuclearization of Africa, and recommends the consideration of steps to give effect to the proposals for the establishment of nuclear-weapon-free zones in the Middle East and South Asia.

Other measures set forth include: early conclusion of an agreement prohibiting the development, production and stockpiling of chemical weapons; a limit on all types of international transfer of conventional weapons; a reduction of military budgets on a mutually agreed basis; and further study of the question of verification of disarmament treaties. The Programme also lists specific measures to be undertaken to mobilize world public opinion on behalf of disarmament.

♦ The section on *Machinery* notes the urgency of revitalizing the existing disarmament machinery and of establishing appropriate forums for disarmament negotiations and deliberations with a more representative character.

In this connection, the General Assembly established, as a deliberative body, a new ***Disarmament Commission*** composed of all United Nations Members. (The Commission established in the early 1950s had not met since 1965.) The Commission's function is to consider and make recommendations on various problems in disarmament. It reports annually to the Assembly.

The Assembly also recognized the continuing requirement for a single multilateral negotiating forum, and it designated the Committee on Disarmament to carry forward the negotiating efforts of its predecessors—the Conference of the Eighteen-Nation Committee on Disarmament (1962-1969) and the Conference of the Committee on Disarmament (1969-1978). The Committee, known since 1984 as the ***Conference on Disarmament***, has 40 members, including all five nuclear-weapon States. It meets at Geneva, for approximately six months each year, and conducts its work by consensus. Its Secretary-General is appointed by the Secretary-General of the United Nations and serves as his personal representative.

As a further result of the first special session, a United Nations programme of fellowships was launched, starting in 1979, in order to train public officials, especially from the developing countries, in disarmament affairs. Twenty-five fellowships are awarded annually. Assistance available under the programme was expanded in 1985 to include new training programmes and advisory services to States in disarmament and security.

In 1979, the Assembly declared the 1980s as the ***Second Disarmament Decade***, stating that the goals of the Decade should remain consistent with the ultimate objective of the disarmament process—namely, general and complete disarmament under effective international control. The goals of the Decade are: the halting and reversing of the arms race; the conclusion of agreements on disarmament according to objectives and priorities of the Final Document of the first special session on disarmament; the strengthening of international peace and security in keeping with the Charter; and the reallocation of resources from military to development purposes, particularly in favour of the developing countries.

The *second special session on disarmament* was held at United Nations Headquarters from 7 June to 10 July 1982. More than 140 States took part in the general debate, putting forward their positions on questions of disarmament, peace and security and expressing concern over the lack of progress on those questions.

Over 60 proposals and position papers by Member States were circulated, dealing with such questions as nuclear disarmament and prevention of war, the banning of chemical weapons, the verification of disarmament agreements and the relationship between disarmament and development. Five draft resolutions were put before the Assembly, containing variously formulated proposals for a nuclear arms freeze, nuclear disarmament and the prevention of nuclear war and for a convention on the prohibition on the use of nuclear weapons; but general agreement could not be reached on any of these proposals and none was pressed to a vote. The Assembly was unable to reach agreement on any specific course of action designed to help halt and reverse the arms race.

In the Concluding Document of the session, however, the Assembly categorically and unanimously reaffirmed the validity of the Final Document of the first special session on disarmament. It expressed its profound preoccupation over the danger of war, particularly nuclear war, and urged Member States to consider as soon as possible proposals designed to secure the avoidance of war, particularly nuclear war. The Assembly also stressed the need for strengthening the central role of the United Nations in the field of disarmament and enhancing the effectiveness of the Conference on Disarmament as the single multilateral negotiating body.

The Assembly decided to launch a *World Disarmament Campaign* to inform, educate and generate public understanding and support for United Nations objectives in arms limitation and disarmament. The Campaign is carried out in all regions of the world and is directed at all segments of the world's population, with primary focus on five major groups: elected representatives, the media, non-governmental organizations, educational communities and research institutions. The observance each year of *Disarmament Week*, beginning on 24 October—*United Nations Day*—was made an integral part of the Campaign.

Since 1982, the Assembly, at its regular sessions, has called for implementation of the recommendations and decisions of the first and second special sessions on disarmament and, in particular, has continued to call for:

⟡ cessation of all test explosions of nuclear weapons, including underground nuclear-weapon tests, and conclusion of a comprehensive nuclear test-ban treaty;

⟡ negotiations on the cessation of the nuclear-arms race and for nuclear disarmament, for conventions prohibiting the use or threat of use of nuclear weapons under any circumstances, and for the prevention of nuclear war;

⟡ a freeze on nuclear weapons by all nuclear-weapon States, particularly the Soviet Union and the United States;

⟡ the establishment of nuclear-weapon-free zones in the Middle East and South Asia, and the implementation of the 1971 *Declaration of the Indian Ocean as a Zone of Peace* and of the *Declaration on the Denuclearization of Africa* adopted by the Organization of African Unity in 1964;

⟡ the conclusion of an international convention on the strengthening of the security of non-nuclear-weapon States against the use or threat of use of nuclear weapons;

⟡ measures to prevent an arms race in outer space;

⟡ the conclusion of conventions on the prohibition of the development, production, stockpiling and use of all chemical, radiological and nuclear neutron weapons;

⟡ agreement on the prohibition of the development and manufacture of new types of weapons of mass destruction and new systems of such weapons; and

⟡ reduction of military budgets and the reallocation of resources now being used for military purposes to economic and social development, particularly for the benefit of the developing countries.

Of course, on issues of such great complexity, which affect the perceived vital security interests of States, the General Assembly's resolutions containing such calls are looked upon by Member States from many different perspectives. Hence, those on substantive disarmament issues are often not adopted unanimously, even though there may be widespread agreement on the desirability of the objectives being sought. Accordingly, efforts towards substantial disarmament have never met with easy success—a situation not likely to see radical rapid change.

Since 1983, the Assembly has, however, called for confidence-building measures, such as greater openness in and information on military and nuclear activities, and security-building measures, such as verifiable limitation and reduction of ground forces and conventional weapons, as well as for co-operation with the Mediterranean States in efforts to reduce tension, promote peace and strengthen security in the region.

In recent years, the Assembly has also increasingly called for studies on various disarmament issues. United Nations disarmament studies have been published on, *inter alia*: disarmament and development (1981); the relationship between disarmament and international security (1982); economic and social consequences of the arms race (1983); conventional disarmament (1984); concepts of security, the naval arms race (1985); and deterrence (1986).

In 1984, the Assembly approved the Statute of the United Nations Institute for Disarmament Research (*see under* Training and research *in* Chapter III). In 1986, it established at Lomé, Togo, a voluntarily funded Regional Centre for Peace and Disarmament in Africa to provide support for disarmament efforts of Member States in that region; a similar Regional Centre for Peace, Disarmament and Development in Latin America is being set up at Lima, Peru.

A third special session on disarmament is scheduled to be held in 1988.

Outer space

United Nations interest in the peaceful uses of outer space was first expressed in 1957, soon after the launching of the first man-made satellite, and has grown steadily with the advance of space technology. The Organization's concern is that space be used for peaceful purposes and that the benefits from space activities be shared by all nations.

The General Assembly's *Committee on the Peaceful Uses of Outer Space*, set up in 1959, is the focal point of United Nations action in this field. Reflecting its interest in both the legal and other aspects of international co-operation regarding outer space, the Committee has a Legal Sub-Committee and a Scientific and Technical Sub-Committee.

Discussions in the Legal Sub-Committee have resulted in five legal instruments, all of which have entered into force:

✧ the 1966 *Treaty on Principles Governing the Activities of States in the Exploration and Use of Outer Space, including the Moon and Other Celestial Bodies* provides that space exploration shall be carried out for the benefit of all countries, irrespective of their degree of economic or scientific development; that outer space shall be the province of all mankind, free for exploration and use by all States on a basis of equality and in accordance with international law, and not subject to national appropriation; and that celestial bodies shall be used exclusively for peaceful purposes. Parties to the Treaty undertake not to place in orbit nuclear weapons, or any other weapons of mass destruction. The Treaty also provides for international responsibility of States parties for all national activities in outer space, whether carried out by governmental agencies or by non-governmental entities;

◇ the 1967 *Agreement on the Rescue of Astronauts, the Return of Astronauts and the Return of Objects Launched into Outer Space* provides for aiding the crews of spacecraft in the event of accident or emergency landing, and establishes procedures for the return of a space object or its components found beyond the territorial limits of the launching authority;

◇ the 1971 *Convention on International Liability for Damage Caused by Space Objects* provides that the launching State is liable for damage caused by its space objects on the earth's surface or to aircraft in flight and also to space objects of another State or persons or property on board;

◇ the 1974 *Convention on the Registration of Objects Launched into Outer Space* provides that launching States shall maintain registries of space objects and furnish specified information on each space object launched, for inclusion in a central United Nations Register;

◇ the 1979 *Agreement Governing Activities of States on the Moon and Other Celestial Bodies* elaborates in more specific terms the principles relating to the moon and other celestial bodies set out in the 1966 Treaty and sets up the basis for the future regulation of exploration and exploitation of natural resources thereof.

Other legal work of the Committee has included elaborating principles on the use of nuclear power sources in outer space, and the studying of definition and delimitation of outer space and the character and utilization of the geostationary orbit.

In 1982, the General Assembly adopted principles governing the use by States of artificial earth satellites for international direct television broadcasting, taking into consideration that such use has international political, economic, social and cultural implications. In 1986, it adopted principles relating to remote sensing of the earth from outer space, which stated that such activities were to be conducted for the benefit of all countries, in accordance with international law, with respect to the sovereignty of all States and peoples over their own natural resources and with respect for the rights and interests of other States. Remote sensing was to be used to protect the earth's natural environment and to protect mankind from natural disasters.

In the scientific and technical fields, the Committee has given priority to the implementation of the United Nations Programme on Space Applications, started in 1969, and the co-ordination of outer space activities within the United Nations system. It also considers and makes recommendations on questions relating to remote sensing of the earth by satellites, the use of nuclear power sources in outer space, space transportation systems and their implications for future activities in space, the physical nature and technical attributes of the geostationary orbit, life sciences (including space medicine), planetary exploration and astronomy, and space communications for development.

Two United Nations–sponsored sounding rocket launching stations—located at Mar del Plata, Argentina, and at Thumba in Kerala, India—provide developing countries with opportunities for practical training and participation in space research for peaceful uses.

Two major conferences on outer space have been organized by the United Nations. The first United Nations Conference on the Exploration and Peaceful Uses of Outer Space (Vienna, 1968) examined the practical benefits to be derived from space research and exploration and the extent to which non-space Powers, especially the developing countries, might enjoy them, and also considered the opportunities available to non-space Powers for international co-operation in space activities.

The Second United Nations Conference on the Exploration and Peaceful Uses of Outer Space (UNISPACE 82), also held at Vienna, in 1982, reflected the growing involvement of all nations, developed and developing, in outer space activities, assessed the current and future state of space science and technology, considered the applications of space technology for economic and social development, and discussed international co-operative programmes related to space and the role of the United Nations.

In its final report, adopted by consensus, UNISPACE 82 stressed that the prevention of an arms race and hostilities in outer space is an essential condition for the promotion and continuation of international co-operation in the exploration and use of outer space for peaceful purposes. It made recommendations on the use of space technology, remote sensing of the earth by satellites, the use of the geostationary orbit, direct television broadcasting by satellites and other matters relating to the peaceful uses of outer space.

The General Assembly, at its 1982 session, endorsed the recommendations of UNISPACE 82, and called for their implementation. The Committee on Outer Space evaluated this implementation.

At subsequent sessions, the Assembly expressed grave concern at the extension of an arms race into outer space and urged all States, in particular those with major space capabilities, to contribute actively to the goal of preventing such an arms race.

Law of the sea

The First United Nations Conference on the Law of the Sea, held at Geneva in 1958, resulted in the adoption of four conventions—on the high seas, on the territorial sea and the contiguous zone, on the continental shelf, and on fishing and conservation of the living resources of the high seas—that were based on drafts prepared by the International Law Commission *(see section on* Progressive development of international law *in* Chapter VI). The Second United Nations Conference on the Law of the Sea, held two years later, made an unsuccessful effort to reach agreement on certain aspects of the territorial sea and fishing zones.

In 1967, the General Assembly decided to establish a committee to study all aspects of the peaceful uses of the sea-bed and its resources beyond the limits of national jurisdiction.

The Sea-Bed Committee began work in 1969 on a statement of legal principles to govern the uses of the sea-bed and its resources, and the following year the Assembly unanimously adopted the Committee's Declaration of Principles, which stated that "the sea-bed and ocean floor, and the subsoil thereof, beyond the limits of national jurisdiction. . . as well as the resources of the area are the common heritage of mankind", to be reserved for peaceful purposes, not subject to national appropriation and not to be explored or exploited except under the international régime to be established.

The Assembly decided in 1970 to convene a new Conference to prepare a single, comprehensive treaty, recognizing that the problems of ocean space are interrelated and needed to be considered as a whole. It was thus to encompass all aspects of the establishment of a régime and machinery for the international sea-bed area, as well as such issues as the régimes of the high seas, the continental shelf and territorial sea (including the question of limits), fishing rights, preservation of the marine environment, scientific research, and access to the sea by land-locked States.

The Third United Nations Conference on the Law of the Sea opened with a brief organizational session in 1973. At its second session (Caracas, 1974), it endorsed the Sea-Bed Committee's recommendation that it work on a new law of the sea treaty as a "package deal", with no one article or section to be approved before all the others were in place. This reflected not only the interdependence of all the issues involved, but also the need to reach a delicate balance of compromises if the final document was to prove viable.

The first informal text was prepared in 1975 as a basis for negotiation. Over the next seven years, in Conference committees and in special negotiating and working groups, the text underwent several major revisions.

The final text of the new Convention was approved by the Conference at United Nations Headquarters on 30 April 1982, by a vote of 130 in favour to 4 against, with 17 abstentions. When it was opened for signature at Montego Bay, Jamaica, on 10 December 1982, the new *United Nations Convention on the Law of the Sea* was signed by 117 States and two other entities—the largest number of signatures ever affixed to a treaty on its first day. By the end of the period of signature, 9 December 1984, the Convention had been signed by 159 States and several other entities (i.e. by the United Nations Council for Namibia on behalf of Namibia, and by the 12-nation European Economic Community, the Cook Islands and Niue). As of 30 June 1987, it had been ratified by 31 States and the Council for Namibia.

The Convention covers almost all ocean space and its uses—navigation and overflight, resource exploration and exploitation, conservation and pollution, fishing and shipping. Its 320 articles and nine annexes constitute a guide for behaviour by States in the world's oceans, defining maritime zones, laying down rules for drawing sea boundaries, assigning legal rights, duties and responsibilities to States and providing machinery for settlement of disputes.

Some of the key features of the Convention are the following:

◇ coastal States would exercise sovereignty over their *territorial sea* of up to 12 nautical miles in breadth, but foreign vessels would be allowed "innocent passage" through those waters for purposes of peaceful navigation;

◇ ships and aircraft of all countries would be allowed "transit passage" through *straits used for international navigation*, as long as they proceeded without delay and without threatening the bordering States; States alongside the straits would be able to regulate navigation and other aspects of passage;

◇ *archipelagic States*, made up of a group or groups of closely related islands and interconnecting waters, would have sovereignty over a sea area enclosed by straight lines drawn between the outermost points of the islands; all other States would enjoy the right of passage through sea lanes designated by the archipelagic States;

◇ coastal States would have sovereign rights in a 200-nautical-mile *exclusive economic zone* with respect to natural resources and certain economic activities, and would exercise jurisdiction over marine science research and environmental protection; all other States would have freedom of navigation and overflight in the zone, as well as freedom to lay submarine cables and pipelines; land-locked and geographically disadvantaged States would have the opportunity to participate in exploiting part of the zone's fisheries on a preferential basis when the coastal State could not harvest them all itself; highly migratory species of fish and marine mammals would be accorded special protection;

◇ coastal States would have sovereign rights over the *continental shelf* (the national area of the sea-bed) for the purpose of exploring and exploiting it; the shelf would extend at least 200 nautical miles from shore, and 350 miles or even more under specified circumstances; coastal States would share with the international community part of the revenue they would derive from exploiting oil and other resources from any part of their shelf beyond 200 miles; a Commission on the Limits of the Continental Shelf would make recommendations to States on the shelf's outer boundaries;

◇ all States would enjoy the traditional freedoms of navigation, overflight, scientific research and fishing on the *high seas*; they would be obliged to adopt, or co-operate with other States in adopting, measures to manage and conserve living resources;

◇ the territorial sea, exclusive economic zone and continental shelf of *islands* would be determined in accordance with rules applicable to land territory, but rocks which could not sustain human habitation or economic life would have no economic zone or continental shelf;

◇ States bordering *enclosed or semi-enclosed seas* would be expected to co-operate on management of living resources and on environmental and research policies and activities;

◇ *land-locked States* would have the right of access to

and from the sea and would enjoy freedom of transit through the territory of transit States;

✧ a "parallel system" would be established for exploring and exploiting the *international sea-bed area*; all activities in the area would be under the control of the International Sea-Bed Authority to be established under the Convention; the Authority would be authorized to conduct its own mining operations through its operating arm, the Enterprise, and also to contract with private and State ventures to give them mining rights in the area, so that they could operate in parallel with the Authority; the first generation of sea-bed prospectors, dubbed "pioneer investors", would have guarantees of production once mining was authorized;

✧ States would be bound to prevent and control *marine pollution* from any source and would be liable for damage caused by violation of their international obligations to combat marine pollution;

✧ all *marine scientific research* in the exclusive economic zone and on the continental shelf would be subject to the consent of the coastal State, but they would in most cases be obliged to grant consent to foreign States when the research was to be conducted for peaceful purposes and fulfilled specified criteria;

✧ States would be bound to promote the *development and transfer of marine technology* "on fair and reasonable terms and conditions", with proper regard for all legitimate interests, including the rights and duties of holders, suppliers and recipients of technology;

✧ States would be obliged to settle by peaceful means their *disputes* over the interpretation or application of the Convention; they would have to submit most types of disputes to a compulsory procedure entailing decisions binding on all parties. Disputes could be submitted to an International Tribunal for the Law of the Sea, to be established under the Convention, to the International Court of Justice, or to arbitration. Conciliation would also be available and, in certain circumstances, submission to it would be compulsory.

With the signing of the Convention on the Law of the Sea in 1982, a Preparatory Commission was established to pave the way for the two major institutions to be set up under the Convention—the International Sea-Bed Authority, with headquarters in Jamaica, and the International Tribunal for the Law of the Sea, to be located in Hamburg, Federal Republic of Germany.

The Commission is to draft rules, regulations and procedures for deep-sea-bed mining and other matters of concern to the future International Sea-Bed Authority and is also to implement a special régime which will allow "pioneer investors" in sea-bed mining development to acquire internationally recognized rights.

Establishment of the Preparatory Commission and of the pioneer investment scheme was provided for in two resolutions adopted by the Third United Nations Conference on the Law of the Sea on 30 April 1982 as part of a package with the Convention.

The Preparatory Commission, beginning in 1983 and meeting twice a year, has worked on elaborating rules for the organs of the International Sea-Bed Authority, and, in four specialized commissions, continued work on: problems that may arise for developing land-based producer States; preparations for the operation of the Enterprise (the mining arm); preparation of a mining code for the exploration and exploitation of the international sea-bed Area; and rules for the International Tribunal for the Law of the Sea.

The Commission has received four applications, from France, India, Japan and the USSR, for the registration of deep-sea-bed mine sites under the special scheme for "pioneer investors". Since there were some overlaps in the claims made—a situation not foreseen by the Conference in 1982—the Commission decided in September 1986 on special arrangements that would facilitate their registration.

Apartheid

Apartheid, as a State-imposed system of institutionalized racial discrimination and segregation, has been practised by South Africa as an official policy since 1948. Under *apartheid*, black South Africans—the overwhelming majority of the people of the country—are denied fundamental rights and liberties. They are not allowed to participate in the political life of the country and are subject to hundreds of repressive laws and regulations. Both the General Assembly and the Security Council have declared *apartheid* incompatible with the Charter of the United Nations. The Assembly has condemned *apartheid* as a crime against humanity, and the Security Council, which has considered the question since 1960, has termed *apartheid* a crime against the conscience and dignity of mankind.

The racial policies of South Africa have been under discussion by the United Nations since 1946, when India complained that South Africa had enacted legislation against South Africans of Indian origin. Beginning in 1952, the wider question of the policies of *apartheid* of the South African Government was included in the General Assembly's agenda.

During the 1950s, the Assembly made repeated appeals to the South African Government to revise its *apartheid* policies in the light of the principles of the Charter. South Africa, however, consistently refused to heed the appeals and resolutions of the General Assembly and the Security Council, viewing the United Nations decisions as illegal and unacceptable and as violating the principle of non-interference in its internal affairs.

The principal United Nations decisions and actions with regard to the question of *apartheid* in South Africa since 1960 are summarized below.

1960 The Security Council met at the request of 29 African and Asian Member States to consider "the situation arising out of the large-scale killings of unarmed and peaceful demonstrators against racial discrimination and segregation" in South Africa. This followed an incident at Sharpeville on 21 March in which South African police fired on peaceful demonstrators protesting the requirement that all Africans carry "reference books"; 69 persons were killed and 180 wounded.

The Council stated that the situation in South Africa had led to international friction and, if continued, might endanger international peace and security. It called on the South African Government to abandon its policy of *apartheid*.

1962 The General Assembly, deploring the failure of South Africa to comply with its repeated requests and demands and those of the Security Council, asked Member States to break off diplomatic relations with South Africa, boycott South African goods, and refrain from all exports to South Africa, including armaments.

The Assembly established a special body, known since 1974 as the ***Special Committee against* Apartheid**, to keep South Africa's racial policies under review, reporting to the Assembly and/or the Security Council. The 18-member intergovernmental Committee was later given a wider mandate to review all aspects of South Africa's *apartheid* policies and their international repercussions.

The Committee conducts hearings, sends missions of consultation, organizes conferences and seminars, and implements United Nations resolutions, particularly by promoting sports, cultural, consumer and other boycotts. With the ***Centre against* Apartheid**, it cooperates with Governments, organizations, trade unions, religious leaders, youth movements and anti-*apartheid* groups in mobilizing international public opinion in support of United Nations resolutions against *apartheid*.

1963 The Security Council instituted a voluntary arms embargo against South Africa, calling on all States to stop the sale and shipment of arms, ammunition of all types and military vehicles to that country. Both the Council and the Assembly asked South Africa to grant unconditional release to all persons imprisoned for having opposed *apartheid*.

1965 The Assembly established the ***United Nations Trust Fund for South Africa***. The Fund is based on voluntary contributions from which grants are made to organizations for legal aid to persons persecuted under South Africa's repressive and discriminatory laws, relief to such persons and their dependants, and relief for refugees from South Africa.

1966 In commemoration of the 1960 Sharpeville incident, the General Assembly proclaimed 21 March as ***International Day for the Elimination of Racial Discrimination***, to be observed annually.

1967 The Assembly established the ***United Nations Educational and Training Programme for Southern Africa***, which grants scholarships to students from South Africa and Namibia for study and training abroad.

1970 The Security Council condemned violations of the arms embargo and called on all States: to strengthen and implement it unconditionally; not to supply vehicles, equipment and spare parts for use by South African military forces and paramilitary groups; to revoke all licences and patents granted for South African manufacture of arms, aircraft or military vehicles; prohibit investment or technical assistance for arms manufacture; and cease all military co-operation with South Africa.

The Assembly urged States to terminate official relations and co-operation with South Africa, and condemned the establishment of and forcible removal of 3 million Africans to the so-called "homelands" (bantustans) as a violation of their inalienable rights.

1972 The Security Council, meeting in Addis Ababa, recognized the legitimacy of the anti-*apartheid* struggle and requested all States to adhere strictly to the arms embargo.

1973 The Assembly adopted the ***International Convention on the Suppression and Punishment of the Crime of* Apartheid** (*see section on* Elimination of racial discrimination *in* Chapter IV). It also established the ***Trust Fund for Publicity against* Apartheid**. The Fund, which became operational in 1975, is used in particular for the wider dissemination of United Nations publicity material on *apartheid* and for the production of audio-visual material on *apartheid*.

1974 The Assembly invited representatives of the South African liberation movements recognized by the Organization of African Unity (OAU)—the African National Congress of South Africa and the Pan Africanist Congress of Azania—to participate as observers in the debates on the question of *apartheid* in the Assembly's Special Political Committee. It later recognized the two organizations as "the authentic representatives of the overwhelming majority of the South African people" and invited them to participate as observers in the debates on the question in the Assembly's plenary meetings.

The Assembly rejected South Africa's credentials and recommended that South Africa be totally excluded from participation in all international organizations and conferences held under United Nations auspices so long as it continued its policies of *apartheid*. Since then, South Africa has not participated in the proceedings of the General Assembly.

1975 The Assembly proclaimed that the United Nations and the international community had a special responsibility towards the oppressed people of South Africa and their liberation movements and towards those imprisoned, restricted or exiled for their struggle against *apartheid*".

1976 The Security Council strongly condemned South Africa's aggression against Angola in March and its attack against Zambia in July as flagrant violations of the sovereignty and territorial integrity of those countries. In both cases, and in a number of other cases since then, the Council demanded that South Africa desist from using the international Territory of Namibia as a base for launching armed attacks against neighbouring African countries and called for international assistance to States bordering South Africa that have suffered economic hardship as a result of their support of United Nations efforts to isolate South Africa.

In June, following the shooting of demonstrators in Soweto, the Council strongly condemned South Africa for its resort to massive violence against and killing of Africans, including schoolchildren. The General Assembly proclaimed 16 June, the day of the uprising, as *International Day of Solidarity with the Struggling People of South Africa*. Later in 1976, it proclaimed 11 October as the *Day of Solidarity with South African Political Prisoners*. Both days are observed annually.

In October, the General Assembly rejected South Africa's declaration of "independence" of the Transkei "homeland", called on all

States not to recognize the Transkei and requested them to prohibit all individuals, corporations and institutions under their jurisdiction from any dealings with any bantustan. Subsequently, the Assembly rejected other "homelands" established as "independent States" by South Africa.

1977 On 4 November, the Security Council made the arms embargo against South Africa mandatory, the first time that such action had been taken against a Member State under Chapter VII of the Charter, which provides for enforcement action in cases such as threats to international peace and security. The Council also decided that States should refrain from any co-operation with that country in the manufacture and development of nuclear weapons. In December, it established a committee to examine implementation by States of the mandatory arms embargo.

The World Conference for Action against *Apartheid*, organized by the Special Committee against *Apartheid* in co-operation with OAU, was held at Lagos in August.

In December, the Assembly adopted the **International Declaration against Apartheid in Sports**, which calls on States to take all appropriate action to cease sporting contacts with any country practising *apartheid* and towards the exclusion or expulsion of any such country from international and regional sports bodies.

The Assembly also asked the Security Council to consider mandatory economic sanctions against South Africa.

1978 *International Anti-Apartheid Year*, proclaimed by the General Assembly, began on 21 March, International Day for the Elimination of Racial Discrimination.

1979 In January, the General Assembly asked the Security Council to consider imposing a mandatory embargo on oil and oil products to South Africa under the United Nations Charter.

1981 The International Conference on Sanctions against South Africa (Paris, May) called for further international action to isolate South Africa, including the imposition of sanctions under Chapter VII of the Charter.

The Assembly decided that 9 August, the anniversary of a 1956 march of women to the government offices in Pretoria in protest over the extension of pass laws to African women, should be observed annually as the *International Day of Solidarity with the Struggle of Women in South Africa and Namibia*.

1982 Proclaimed as *International Year of Mobilization for Sanctions against South Africa* by the Assembly in 1981, the Year was aimed at mobilizing world public opinion in support of comprehensive and mandatory sanctions against South Africa and of encouraging action by States, individually and collectively. To achieve those objectives, a number of conferences and seminars were held in different parts of the world, including the Asian Regional Conference for Action against *Apartheid*, which adopted the Manila Declaration for Action against *Apartheid*. On the Day of Solidarity with South African Political Prisoners, the Special Committee against *Apartheid* launched a world-wide campaign for the release of South African political prisoners.

1983 Conferences to promote further international action against *apartheid* included the Latin American Regional Conference for Action against *Apartheid*, which adopted the Caracas Declaration on Action against *Apartheid*; the International Conference on Sanctions against *Apartheid* in Sports held at London; and the International Conference on the Alliance between South Africa and Israel, held at Vienna.

The General Assembly rejected "constitutional proposals" endorsed in 1983 by South Africa and all manœuvres to entrench white minority rule and *apartheid*. It declared "that only the total eradication of *apartheid* and the establishment of a non-racial democratic society based on majority rule, through the full and free exercise of adult suffrage by all the people in a united and non-fragmented South Africa, can lead to a just and lasting solution of the explosive situation in South Africa".

1984 In June, the Special Committee against *Apartheid* held, in New York, the North American Conference for Action against *Apartheid*, and, in August, in Tunis, the Conference of Arab Solidarity with the Struggle for Liberation in Southern Africa, among others.

The General Assembly rejected the South African Constitution that created a racially segregated tricameral Parliament, including Asians and Coloureds but excluding Africans.

1985 In March, the Security Council condemned the Pretoria régime for the killing of defenceless African people protesting against their forced removal, as well as arbitrary arrests of members of organizations opposed to *apartheid*.

The International Conference on Women under *Apartheid* (Arusha, United Republic of Tanzania, May), promoted further material and moral assistance to women and children and the struggle for national liberation.

The International Conference on *Apartheid* in Sports (Paris, May) adopted a declaration strengthening the sports boycott against South

Africa. The boycott was further strengthened in December by the General Assembly, which adopted the *International Convention against* **Apartheid** *in Sports*. The treaty obliges States parties not to permit sports contacts with countries practising *apartheid*.

The Security Council has condemned several attacks by South African forces on neighbouring States, and has demanded the immediate and unconditional cessation of such acts of aggression and the withdrawal from the territory of independent States. It asked the Secretary-General to send a mission to Botswana in July and August to assess damage there, and in September it appointed a three-member Commission of Investigation for a similar purpose in Angola. It called for compensation to those countries for the damage done. In accordance with a December resolution of the Council, the Secretary-General appointed a Representative in Lesotho to keep him informed of developments affecting that country's territorial integrity.

In July, the Council condemned the establishment of a state of emergency imposed that month in 36 South African districts, and demanded that it be lifted. It uged Member States to adopt such measures as suspending all new investment in South Africa, prohibiting the sale of coins minted there, restricting sports and cultural relations, suspending guaranteed export loans, prohibiting all new nuclear contracts, and prohibiting sales of computer equipment that could be used by the army or police.

1986 The World Conference on Sanctions against Racist South Africa (June, Paris) reviewed developments since the 1981 Paris Conference on sanctions, and called for comprehensive and mandatory sanctions against South Africa aimed at bringing an end to that country's *apartheid* system, to its illegal occupation of Namibia and to its attacks on neighbouring States.

Also in June, the Council issued a statement condemning the imposition of the nation-wide state of emergency in South Africa and called for it to be lifted immediately.

Efforts in the Council in July to make mandatory such "selective economic and other sanctions" as those it had urged States to adopt a year earlier—and several subsequent efforts as well—were not successful. However, to close loopholes, reinforce and make the arms embargo more comprehensive, the Council in November urged States to ensure that components of and spare parts for embargoed items did not reach the South African military or police forces through third countries, and asked States to investigate violations and prevent circumventions of the arms embargo.

In November also, the General Assembly urged the United Kingdom and the United States and others opposed to applying comprehensive and mandatory sanctions to reassess their position. It also set up an Intergovernmental Group to Monitor the Supply and Shipping of Oil and Petroleum Products to South Africa.

1987 In April, the Security Council expressed deep concern about a South African decree of 10 April prohibiting nearly all forms of protest against detentions without trial or support for detainees, and called on South Africa to revoke it.

CHAPTER III

The United Nations at work for economic and social development

Most of the work of the United Nations, measured in terms of money and personnel, goes into programmes aimed at achieving economic and social progress in the developing countries, where two thirds of the world's people live, often in the grip of poverty, hunger, ignorance and disease.

Since its early days, the United Nations, carrying out the pledge in Article 55 of its Charter to "promote higher standards of living, full employment and conditions of economic and social progress and development", has supported the development efforts of the poorer countries.

Beginning in 1960, the General Assembly proclaimed three successive United Nations Development Decades in order to focus international action on concrete programmes to aid developing countries. The Assembly has also adopted declarations, programmes of action and development strategies, designed to strengthen international co-operation for development.

In the 1960s, both the General Assembly and the Economic and Social Council increasingly stressed the need for a unified approach to economic and social planning to promote balanced and sound development. This emphasis on unified development is reflected in the provisions of the *Declaration on Social Progress and Development*, adopted by the Assembly in 1969.

Other Assembly resolutions calling for a unified approach to development analysis and planning were adopted in 1983 and 1986. On the occasion of the twentieth anniversary of the adoption of the Declaration on Social Progress and Development, in 1989, the Secretary-General is to report on the status of its implementation and on possible ways and means of increasing the contribution of the relevant parts of the United Nations system towards achieving the full realization of the principles and objectives contained in it.

New international economic order

Before the end of the *First United Nations Development Decade* (1961-1970), the need for a world plan of action or "strategy" for development became evident, and the General Assembly therefore adopted, in 1970, an International Development Strategy for the *Second United Nations Development Decade* (1971-1980), which set targets for progress and measures for achieving specific goals. The unanimous adoption of the International Development Strategy for the Second Development Decade was an important step in the promotion of international economic co-operation on a just and equitable basis.

Four years later, on 1 May 1974, at a special session on development, the General Assembly adopted the *Declaration and Programme of Action on the Establishment of a New International Economic Order*. Member States solemnly proclaimed their determination to work urgently for "the establishment of a new international economic order based on equity, sovereignty, interdependence, common interest and co-operation among States, irrespective of their economic and social systems", which would "correct inequalities and redress existing injustices, make it possible to eliminate the widening gap between the developed and the developing countries and ensure steadily accelerating economic and social development in peace and justice for present and future generations".

To promote further the establishment of a new international economic order, the Assembly adopted, in December 1974, the *Charter of Economic Rights and Duties of States*. The Charter stipulates that every State has the right freely to exercise full permanent sovereignty over its wealth and natural resources, to regulate foreign investments within its national jurisdiction, and to nationalize, expropriate or transfer the ownership of foreign property, and it provides that appropriate compensation should be paid in cases of nationalization and that any controversies should be settled under the domestic laws of the nationalizing States unless all States concerned agree to other peaceful means.

Measures to implement both the new international economic order and the Charter of Economic Rights and Duties of States have not enjoyed the same relative consensus as did their original adoption. Efforts to establish follow-up mechanisms for each have not yielded significant progress in recent years.

At another special session on development and international economic co-operation, held in September 1975, the General Assembly specified further measures to serve as the basis for concrete negotiations to be held within the United Nations system, with the participation of all States and within a specified time-frame, and to include major issues in the field of raw materials, energy, trade, development, money and finance. The Assembly also called for a restructuring of the economic and social sectors of the United Nations system so as to make it more fully capable of dealing with problems of international economic co-operation and development in a comprehensive and effective manner.

In 1979, the General Assembly called for the launching, at the third special session on development in 1980, of a round of global and sustained negotiations on international economic co-operation for development. The global negotiations called for by the Assembly did not achieve the hoped-for progress at the special session held in September 1980, but at the Assembly's regular session that year, an International Development Strategy for the Third United Nations Development Decade was adopted by consensus.

Although agreement has not been reached on the procedures and agenda for the global negotiations, the Assembly has kept open its agenda item on launching them while informal consultations continue.

International Development Strategy for the Third United Nations Development Decade

The International Development Strategy for the Third United Nations Development Decade, adopted by the General Assembly on 5 December 1980, states that in an interdependent world economy, problems such as high inflation and unemployment, prolonged monetary instability and intensified protectionist pressures cannot be solved without resolving the particular problems facing the developing countries, and that accelerated development of developing countries is of vital importance for the steady growth of the world economy and essential for world peace and stability.

The Strategy for the Decade sets forth specific goals and objectives for an accelerated development of the developing countries in the period 1981-1990. It also sets out a series of policy measures—in international trade, industrialization, food and agriculture, financial resources for development, international monetary and financial issues, science and technology for development, energy, transport, environment, human settlements, disaster relief and social development, as well as in technical co-operation, including co-operation among developing countries themselves, and special measures for the least developed countries and for geographically disadvantaged developing countries such as island and land-locked countries.

In mid-decade, a *Committee on the Review and Appraisal of the Implementation of the International Development Strategy for the Third United Nations Development Decade*, in the set of agreed conclusions it adopted and which the Assembly endorsed in 1985, reaffirmed the goals and objectives of the Strategy and renewed the commitments to give effect to its policy measures. The document singled out for special attention, for example, trade, the international monetary system, international debt, and access to financial resources, and indicated broad guidelines for future action. It noted that key targets had not been met, though there was modest progress in certain areas. The full dimension of the critical situation in sub-Saharan Africa had not been foreseen, nor was the coalescing of adverse factors that had brought on the international debt crisis.

Concern by the United Nations system as a whole and by its Member States over the critical economic situation in Africa led to the convening in May 1986 of a General Assembly special session on Africa—the first time the Assembly had devoted a special session to a specific region *(see section below on* Disaster relief and special economic assistance).

In 1986, the Assembly also sought to strengthen international economic co-operation for resolving external debt problems of developing countries. By an Assembly resolution on this subject, Member States recognized the severe and continuing burden placed on many developing countries by debt-servicing problems and agreed on a number of elements aimed at alleviating them.

United Nations programmes for economic and social development

The United Nations family—the United Nations itself and the various organizations and agencies related to it—is united in a global effort for the economic and social development of the developing countries, through programmes ranging from technical co-operation, to surveys and studies, to the convening of international conferences, and from comprehensive development planning to specific projects in individual fields such as trade, industry and agriculture.

To help Governments establish a more effective framework for growth, the United Nations offers aid in the preparation of national development plans to ensure balanced economic and social growth and the best use of available financial, physical and human resources. It helps developing countries mobilize the funds needed to pay for development programmes, both by increasing their own export earnings and by attracting outside capital at terms they can afford.

Increasing priority is being given to programmes for resource development, the application of science and technology to development and the exploitation of new and renewable sources of energy. The United Nations helps Governments investigate and make maximum use of natural resources, modernize and expand transport and communications facilities and improve national statistical, budgetary and administrative services.

Other fields in which the United Nations family is helping developing countries include population assistance, housing and community development, land reform and protection of the environment.

The United Nations also has programmes geared to population groups—children, youth, women, the elderly, the disabled and refugees—and programmes of special social concern, such as drug abuse control and crime prevention.

Development projects for individual countries are carried out at the request of the Governments concerned. Other programmes are implemented on a regional basis, by the United Nations economic commissions—for Africa, for Asia and the Pacific, for Western Asia, for Latin America and the Caribbean, and for Europe. Still other questions, of global concern, call for the convening of international conferences with world-wide representation. Among such global conferences convened in recent years are the following:

- ◇ United Nations Conference on Desertification (Nairobi, 1977);
- ◇ United Nations Water Conference (Mar del Plata, 1977);
- ◇ United Nations Conference on Technical Co-operation among Developing Countries (Buenos Aires, 1978);
- ◇ United Nations Conference on Science and Technology for Development (Vienna, 1979);
- ◇ World Conference on Agrarian Reform and Rural Development (Rome, 1979);
- ◇ World Conference on the United Nations Decade for Women: Equality, Development and Peace (Copenhagen, 1980);
- ◇ United Nations Conference on New and Renewable Sources of Energy (Nairobi, 1981);

◇ United Nations Conference on the Least Developed Countries (Paris, 1981);

◇ World Assembly on Aging (Vienna, 1982);

◇ International Conference on Population (Mexico City, 1984);

◇ World Conference to Review and Appraise the Achievements of the United Nations Decade for Women (Nairobi, 1985);

◇ United Nations Conference for the Promotion of International Co-operation in the Peaceful Uses of Nuclear Energy (Geneva, 1987);

◇ International Conference on Drug Abuse and Illicit Trafficking (Vienna, 1987);

◇ United Nations Conference on Trade and Development (Belgrade, 1983; Geneva, 1987).

On the pages which follow, the various programmes of the United Nations family of organizations in support of economic and social development are briefly outlined. The activities of the intergovernmental agencies related to the United Nations are described in Chapter VII.

Technical co-operation for development

The United Nations and its family of organizations and agencies have long played a key role in providing technical co-operation to stimulate development. The International Development Strategy for the Third United Nations Development Decade and subsequent decisions of intergovernmental bodies call for a renewed emphasis on technical co-operation and a significant increase in the resources provided for this purpose. It recognizes that technical co-operation makes an essential contribution to the efforts of developing countries to achieve self-reliance through its broad role of facilitating and supporting investment, human resources development, research and training, among other things.

Funding for United Nations technical co-operation comes from the United Nations regular programme of technical co-operation, the United Nations Development Programme (UNDP), the United Nations Fund for Population Activities (UNFPA) and other extrabudgetary resources, which include projects financed by contributions provided directly to the executing agencies by multilateral funding organizations within or outside the United Nations system, other than UNDP, and by unilateral or bilateral contributions from Governments and non-governmental organizations.

In order to consolidate under one authority the responsibilities and resources within the United Nations Secretariat in support of technical co-operation activities, the General Assembly, in March 1978, set up the *Department of Technical Co-operation for Development (DTCD)*. As an executing agency for UNDP and UNFPA and as a principal operational arm of the Secretariat, DTCD executes projects financed from the regular programme of technical co-operation and from extrabudgetary sources, providing technical expertise, training materials and direct advisory assistance to Governments in the formulation, implementation and evaluation of country and intercountry programmes and specific projects.

United Nations technical co-operation programmes and projects help Governments establish a more effective framework for growth by aiding:

◇ in the preparation of comprehensive plans to promote balanced economic and social development and the best use of available financial, physical and human resources;

◇ in the exploration, exploitation and effective use of natural resources, such as water, minerals and energy supplies; and

◇ in the improvement of national statistical and public administration systems.

Technical co-operation programmes and projects also focus on population questions, including integration of population policies in development planning, and on the rehabilitation and development of housing, urban facilities and social services. Moreover, aid is offered in community development, to improve living conditions in both rural and urban areas; in addressing land reform problems; and in efforts to deal more effectively with youth problems.

Other United Nations efforts for economic and social advancement include studies to compile information and analyse needs, and conferences at which experience is pooled and intergovernmental agreements may be drawn up—on trade questions, for example.

Activities which meet needs on a regional level are carried out by the five regional commissions—for Africa, Asia and the Pacific, Western Asia, Latin America and the Caribbean, and Europe—aimed at strengthening economic relations within and outside the regions and furthering their economic and social development.

✻ ✻ ✻ ✻

The **United Nations Development Programme (UNDP)** is the world's largest channel for multilateral technical and pre-investment co-operation. It is active in more than 150 developing countries and territories. Its five-year country and intercountry programmes co-ordinate development activities in virtually every economic and social sector, including farming, fishing, forestry, mining, manufacturing, power, transport, communications, housing and building, trade and tourism, health and environmental sanitation, education and training, community development, economic planning and public administration.

There are some 5,000 UNDP-supported projects currently in operation, valued at some $7.5 billion. Eighty per cent of UNDP's country programme funds are directed to countries with an annual per capita income of $750 or less. With ready access to the talent bank of the 36 participating and executing agencies of the United Nations development system, and of research institutes in every field, UNDP can tap the most comprehensive and advanced sources of technical assistance available.

UNDP projects, which are aimed at helping developing countries make better use of their human and natural resources, improve living standards, expand productivity and contribute more fully to an expanding world economy, involve:

✧ carrying out surveys and feasibility studies to determine the availability and economic value of a country's natural resources and to assess other potentials for increased output and wider distribution of goods and services;

✧ expanding and strengthening educational systems through university level, and supporting a full spectrum of professional, vocational and technical instruction, from work-oriented literacy training to fellowships for specialized studies abroad;

✧ establishing facilities for applying modern technological research methods to priority development problems and for disseminating new discoveries and production techniques; and

✧ upgrading capabilities for economic and social development planning.

UNDP also plays a catalytic role by helping to mobilize the capital investments required and lays the groundwork for follow-up capital investment. Over the past 25 years, UNDP-financed activities have stimulated nearly $89 billion in follow-up investment from public and private sources.

UNDP's mandate also enables it to assist developing countries with "high risk" ventures and support activities for which funding from other sources is not readily available.

In all these areas, UNDP works to broaden economic and technical co-operation among the developing countries themselves. It has pioneered efforts to involve increasing numbers of donors and beneficiaries in the development process; increased participation of the private sector is also a priority. It is also addressing the role of women in all UNDP projects and promoting co-operation between UNDP and non-governmental organizations.

Major issues which preoccupied the development community in the past two years were the developing countries' external debt problems; their acute need to shape and implement structural adjustment policies; recovery from the drought and famine in Africa; increasing agricultural productivity; and enhancing management efficiency of government institutions and enterprises.

UNDP assistance is rendered only at the request of Governments and in response to their priority needs, integrated into overall national and regional plans.

UNDP also administers a number of special purpose funds and programmes, including: the *United Nations Capital Development Fund*, which provides grants and long-term loans for grassroots self-help activities in some of the world's poorest countries; the *Special Measures Fund for Least Developed Countries*, which provides technical assistance to build up the planning, policy analysis and co-ordination capacities of the poorest countries; the *United Nations Revolving Fund for Natural Resources Exploration*; the *United Nations Trust Fund for Sudano-Sahelian Activities*; the *United Nations Volunteers* programme; the *United Nations Development Fund for Women*; and the *United Nations Fund for Science and Technology for Development* (see under related subject headings below).

UNDP is financed by voluntary contributions from Governments of Member States of the United Nations and its related agencies.

* * * *

Established by the General Assembly in 1971, the **United Nations Volunteers (UNV)** programme—the only volunteer-sending programme in the United Nations system—is administered by UNDP.

UNV channels professionally qualified men and women volunteers into development co-operation activities calling for middle-level and upper-middle-level expertise. The volunteers serve in both UNDP- and United Nations-assisted projects, as well as development programmes carried out directly by host Governments. Recruited globally, they are sent to a country only at the request, and with the approval, of the host Government.

Volunteers currently encompass over 150 professions—for the most part practitioners sharing skills at the working level, rather than theoreticians or advisers. Two-year contracts offer a monthly allowance adequate for necessities rather than a salary commensurate with qualifications and experience.

Through its Domestic Development Services programme, UNV supports indigenous organizations which promote self-reliance in development through grass-roots participation. Since 1976, UNV has also been a major operational unit for executing youth programmes, especially pilot projects to enhance the participation of youth in development activities.

In recognition of the important contribution of volunteer service to development activities, 5 December is observed annually as *International Volunteer Day for Economic and Social Development.*

Trade and development

The first **United Nations Conference on Trade and Development (UNCTAD),** held at Geneva in the spring of 1964, led to the establishment of UNCTAD as a permanent organ of the General Assembly in December of that year. Sessions of the Conference are held every few years—in 1968 (New Delhi), 1972 (Santiago), 1976 (Nairobi), 1979 (Manila), 1983 (Belgrade) and 1987 (Geneva).

One of UNCTAD's principal functions is the negotiation and adoption of multilateral legal instruments in the field of international trade. Since its establishment, a number of such instruments have been negotiated and adopted under its auspices, beginning in 1964 with the General and Special Principles to govern international trade relations and trade policies conducive to development.

One of UNCTAD's major programmes aims at securing remunerative, equitable and stable prices for the primary commodities on which developing countries depend heavily for export earnings. Central to the programme, known as the Integrated Programme for Commodities, is the negotiation of fixed-term agreements on specific commodities—those currently in force concern natural rubber (1987), cocoa (1986), olive oil (1986) and tin (1981). These agreements have as their principal objective the stabilization of conditions in the international trade of the commodities concerned and, for this purpose, establish pricing and supply arrangements. The rubber and tin agreements provide, for the first time in history, for mandatory financing of buffer stocks by producers and consumers. Development-type agreements which came into force in 1984 and 1985 concern jute (1982) and tropical timber (1983).

An important element of the Integrated Programme for Commodities is the Agreement Establishing the Common Fund for Commodities, which was adopted by the United Nations Negotiating Conference on a Common Fund in 1980. The Common Fund, which has been ratified by the required 90 States, will enter into force when ratifying States represent two thirds of the Fund's directly contributed capital of $470 million. The Fund will establish a new multilateral financial institution aimed at facilitating the conclusion and functioning of international commodity agreements, particularly concerning commodities of special interest to developing countries.

Other multilateral agreements in the field of international trade negotiated by UNCTAD include:

 ✧ the *Convention on a Code of Conduct for Liner Conferences* (1974), which establishes rules concerning the operation of liner shipping, in particular as regards the loading rights of national shipping lines in respect of liner cargoes generated by their countries' foreign trade;

 ✧ the *Set of Multilaterally Agreed Equitable Principles and Rules for the Control of Restrictive Business Practices* (1980), which establishes, for the first time, international means for the control of restrictive business practices, including those of transnational corporations, adversely affecting international trade, in particular the trade and economic development of developing countries;

 ✧ the *United Nations Convention on International Multimodal Transport of Goods* (1980), which establishes a legal régime for the contract of such goods; and

 ✧ the *United Nations Convention on Conditions for Registration of Ships* (1986), which introduces new standards of responsibility and accountability in world shipping and defines the elements of genuine linkage that should exist between a ship and the State whose flag it flies.

Negotiations have been in progress since 1978 on an International Code of Conduct on the Transfer of Technology.

At the beginning of the decade, UNCTAD launched a Substantial New Programme of Action for the 1980s for the least-developed countries, to transform their economies, aiming at self-sustained development and minimum standards of nutrition, health, transport and communications, housing, education and job opportunities.

The executive body of UNCTAD is the **Trade and Development Board**, which normally meets twice a year. Several permanent committees report to the Board with their recommendations on specific areas of trade with which they deal: commodities; economic co-operation among developing countries; invisibles and financing; manufacturing; shipping; transfer of technology; and trade preferences.

Transnational corporations and the world economy

The importance of transnational corporations in the world economy is shown by the fact that direct foreign investment by 20,000 companies totalled nearly $700 billion in 1986; approximately half that sum was accounted for by only about 50 corporations. Sales by transnationals' foreign affiliates accounted for more than 40 per cent of total sales in the 1980s (up from 30 per cent in the early 1970s), and about one third of world trade was intra-firm trade conducted by the same corporation.

In 1974, the Economic and Social Council created the **Commission on Transnational Corporations** and the **United Nations Centre on Transnational Corporations** to serve as focal points within the United Nations Secretariat for all matters related to transnational corporations. The Centre acts as the secretariat to the 48-member Commission and, since 1983, to its special session entrusted with negotiating a code of conduct on transnational corporations. It also provides support to the Intergovernmental Working Group of Experts on International Standards of Accounting and Reporting.

The work of the Centre and its joint units (which it has with each of the regional commissions) falls into three main categories:

✧ *normative activities*, involving assisting intergovernmental bodies in creating basic rules to govern interaction between transnational corporations and host Governments. Most important among these is the code of conduct, seeking to define the rights and responsibilities of both transnationals and Governments in the interest of a stable, predictable and mutually beneficial investment relationship. The Centre also assists in harmonizing standards for information disclosure by corporations with transnational operations.

◆ *research* on patterns and trends in international investment flows and in the international system of production developed through transnational corporations. This work is captured in the quinquennial survey of transnationals in world development. Other areas of research include: the role of transnational corporations in banking, trade, insurance, advertising and transborder data flows; transnationals in South Africa and Namibia; and the impact of transnationals on health and the environment. The Centre collects and analyses data, including model contracts, laws and regulations.

◆ *technical co-operation*, providing advisory and information services to aid developing countries in their dealings with transnational corporations. Assistance is offered in drafting and revising policies, law and regulations and in evaluating and formulating foreign direct investment and technology projects, drawing on multidisciplinary teams of experts. The Centre also conducts training workshops, seminars and round-tables for host-developing-country officials, members of parastatal enterprises and private sector entrepreneurs on developing country/transnational corporation interactions.

Science and technology for development

A major event of the first United Nations Development Decade (1960s) was the United Nations Conference on the Application of Science and Technology for the Benefit of the Less Developed Countries (Geneva, 1963). The Conference focused world attention on the practical possibilities of accelerating development through the application of advances in science and technology and on the need for reorienting research towards the requirements of the developing countries.

A second conference, the United Nations Conference on Science and Technology for Development (Vienna, 1979), adopted a Programme of Action designed to put science and technology to work for the economic development of all countries, particularly the developing countries. It recommended the creation of a high-level intergovernmental committee on science and technology for development and the establishment of a voluntary fund to finance activities in this field.

The Programme of Action consists of 65 recommendations divided into three target areas: the first deals with strengthening the science and technology capacities of developing countries; the second concerns restructuring existing patterns of international scientific and technological relations; and the third contains recommendations for strengthening the role of the United Nations system in science and technology and the provision of increased financial resources.

Endorsing the recommendations of the Vienna Conference in 1979, the General Assembly established an *Intergovernmental Committee on Science and Technology for Development*, open to all States, to draw up policy guidelines, monitor activities within the United Nations system, promote implementation of the Vienna Programme, identify priorities and assess development, and mobilize resources. The Assembly also created within the United Nations Secretariat a *Centre for Science and Technology for Development* to provide the necessary substantive support to the Committee and to co-ordinate activities at the secretariat level within the United Nations system.

In 1982, the Assembly established long-term arrangements for the United Nations Financing System for Science and Technology for Development to finance a broad range of activities intended to strengthen the endogenous scientific and technological capacities of developing countries. In 1986, it transferred the responsibilities and resources of the System to a newly created *United Nations Fund for Science and Technology for Development*, administered by UNDP.

Natural resources and energy

In a 1952 resolution, the General Assembly declared that developing countries had "the right to determine freely the use of their natural resources" and that they must use such resources towards realizing their economic development plans in accordance with their national interests.

The importance of natural resources for economic development was further emphasized in 1970, when the Economic and Social Council established the *Committee on Natural Resources*. The Committee develops guidelines for advisory services to Governments, reviews arrangements to co-ordinate United Nations activities in natural resources development and evaluates trends and salient issues concerning natural resources exploration and development, as well as prospects for selected energy, water and mineral resources.

During the 1970s, the Committee on Natural Resources played a central role in focusing world attention on another crisis—the status of the global stock of water resources to meet human, commercial and agricultural needs. As a result of an initiative of the Committee, the United Nations Water Conference was convened in 1977 in Mar del Plata, Argentina. The Conference adopted the Mar del Plata Action Plan to guide international efforts effectively to manage, develop and use water resources. Giving impetus to the Action Plan, the General Assembly, in 1980, launched the *International Drinking Water Supply and Sanitation Decade* (1981-1990). An Interregional Symposium on Improved Efficiency in the Management of Water Resources: Follow-up to the Mar del Plata Action Plan (New York, January 1987) discussed the progress of implementation during the decade since the Water Conference.

In 1973, the General Assembly established the *United Nations Revolving Fund for Natural Resources Exploration*, which began operation in 1975. The Fund is financed from voluntary contributions and is intended to provide additional risk capital for mineral exploration in developing countries. In 1981, the Fund was authorized to extend its exploration activities to geothermal energy.

During the 1970s, with the rise and volatility of costs for petroleum which affected the economies of all countries, particularly those of the poorer countries, and the growing awareness that known supplies of petroleum would, in the long run, be unable to meet global requirements, more attention was focused on new and renewable sources of energy.

This led to the General Assembly's decision to convene the United Nations Conference on New and Renewable Sources of Energy (Nairobi, August 1981). The Conference examined different alternative forms of energy, including solar energy, biomass energy, wind power, hydropower, fuelwood and charcoal, geothermal energy, ocean energy, oil shale and tar sands, peat and the use of draught animals for energy purposes. It adopted the Nairobi Programme of Action for the Development and Utilization of New and Renewable Sources of Energy, a blueprint for national and international action.

Endorsing the Nairobi Programme later that year, the Assembly set up an interim committee to launch immediate implementation of the Programme, and, in 1982, established the *Committee on the Development and Utilization of New and Renewable Sources of Energy*, open to the participation of all States as full members.

Addressing another area of significance in the energy field— nuclear energy for the economic and social development of developing countries—the Assembly in 1977 set in motion arrangements for an international conference on the subject, the first global effort in this field, the United Nations Conference for the Promotion of International Co-operation in the Peaceful Uses of Nuclear Energy (Geneva, 1987). Although unable to reach agreement on principles acceptable

84

to all, the high-level participants expressed views and exchanged experience on topics ranging from the production of electricity to the various applications of nuclear techniques in food and agriculture, medicine, hydrology, research and industry.

Protection of the environment

The first United Nations Conference on the Human Environment was held in Stockholm in June 1972, following a 1968 decision of the General Assembly that action at the national, regional and international levels was needed to limit the impairment of the human environment and protect and improve man's natural surroundings.

The Conference adopted the ***Declaration on the Human Environment***, which proclaims the right of human beings to a quality environment and their responsibility to protect and improve the environment for future generations. It also adopted an Action Plan, containing over 100 recommendations for measures to be taken by Governments and international organizations to protect life, control contamination from man-made pollutants and improve cities and other human settlements.

The opening day of the Conference, 5 June, is commemorated annually as ***World Environment Day***.

Later in 1972, on the basis of the Conference's recommendations, the General Assembly created the **United Nations Environment Programme (UNEP)** to monitor significant changes in the environment and to encourage and co-ordinate sound environmental practices. The first United Nations agency to be based in a developing country, UNEP has its headquarters in Nairobi.

UNEP's programmes include "Earthwatch", an international surveillance network with three main components: a Global Environmental Monitoring System, which monitors selected environmental parameters to provide Governments with the information necessary to understand, anticipate and combat adverse environmental changes, whether man-made or natural; INFOTERRA, a computerized referral service to 20,000 sources in some 100 countries for environmental information and expertise; and the International Register of Potentially Toxic Chemicals, which works through a network of national correspondents to provide scientific and regulatory information on chemicals that may be dangerous to health and the environment.

Other major programmes of UNEP include implementation, in the Sudano-Sahelian region of Africa, of the Plan of Action to Combat

Desertification, adopted by the United Nations Conference on Desertification (Nairobi, 1977). The Plan comprises integrated national and international programmes of land reclamation and management.

A UNEP committee co-operated closely with a special commission of experts on environment and development, established in 1984 to prepare long-term integrated environmental strategies for a world Environmental Perspective to the Year 2000 and Beyond. The Governing Council, UNEP's executive body, endorsed the Perspective in 1987.

UNEP's efforts against marine pollution, begun with a pilot programme in the Mediterranean, now also include anti-marine pollution programmes for the Kuwait region, the Red Sea and the Gulf of Aden, the Wider Caribbean, East, West and Central Africa, the East Asian Seas and the South Pacific.

In environmental law, UNEP has developed guidelines and principles regarding the harmonious utilization by States of shared natural resources and offshore mining and drilling. Culminating almost eight years of UNEP efforts, the international *Convention for the Protection of the Ozone Layer* was adopted at a Vienna conference in 1985. It will enter into force after 20 States have ratified or accepted it. Other important activities include the preparation of regional conventions for the protection of the marine environment, and related technical protocols.

UNEP has supported pilot projects for producing energy from the sun, wind and household and agricultural wastes, as well as a comprehensive study on the environmental impact of the production, use and transport of various types of energy. It also promotes technical assistance, education and training for management of the environment.

At a special session in 1982, the Governing Council reviewed the environmental achievements and shortcomings of the international community since Stockholm and charted the main lines of action for UNEP in the 1980s. The Declaration of Nairobi, adopted at that session, sets out the major problems to be addressed by Governments, international agencies and the public at large, and reaffirms the commitment of Governments to the objectives and principles of the Stockholm Plan of Action and Declaration.

Human settlements

United Nations concern with the problems of human settlements, particularly with the deteriorating quality of living conditions and the need to link urban and regional development programmes with national plans, led to the convening of the first international conference on the subject—Habitat: United Nations Conference on Human Settlements (Vancouver, May/June 1976).

The Declaration and Plan of Action adopted by the Conference represented an important commitment by Governments and the international community to improve the quality of life for all people through human settlements development. The Plan of Action contains 64 recommendations for national action concerning settlements policies, settlement planning, provision of shelter, infrastructure and services, land use and land tenure, the role of public participation, and effective institutions and management.

Annually, the first Monday in October is *World Habitat Day*, the first observance of which, in 1986, marked the tenth anniversary year of the Conference.

Acting on a recommendation of the Conference, the General Assembly decided in 1977 to transform the Committee on Housing, Building and Planning into a *Commission on Human Settlements*, and in 1978 it established the **United Nations Centre for Human Settlements (Habitat)**, with headquarters in Nairobi, to serve as a focal point for human settlements action and to co-ordinate human settlements activities within the United Nations system.

The Centre's major areas of concern include provision of technical co-operation to government programmes, organization of expert meetings, workshops and training seminars, publication of technical documents and dissemination of information throughout the world.

Technical co-operation projects in developing countries cover such areas as national settlement policies and programmes, urban and regional planning, rural and urban housing and infrastructure development, slum upgrading and sites-and-services schemes, low-cost building technology, technologies for urban and rural water supply and sanitation systems, and the establishment or strengthening of government institutions concerned with human settlements.

In 1982, the General Assembly proclaimed 1987 the *International Year of Shelter for the Homeless*. The objectives of the Year were to improve the shelter situation of the poor and disadvantaged at both individual and community levels, particularly in developing countries, both before and during 1987, and to demonstrate means of continuing those efforts as on-going national programmes beyond 1987. The Year's activities were to be formally integrated into the Centre's work programme at the end of 1987.

World food problems

While the United Nations has long been involved in working towards solutions to the age-old problem of food shortages, in 1974 a major effort was launched to tackle food crisis situations that had developed in many parts of the world. The United Nations World Food Conference (Rome, November 1974) called on the General Assembly to establish a 36-nation ministerial-level **World Food Council (WFC)** to review annually major problems and policy issues affecting the world food situation and to bring its political influence to bear on Governments and United Nations bodies and agencies alike.

The Council's approach to solving world food problems and eliminating hunger is to encourage the adoption—by developing countries, where most of the world's estimated 730 million hungry people live and which do not produce enough to feed their populations—of national food strategies. Under this plan, each country assesses its current food situation—needs, supply, potential for increasing food production (including land and its distribution), storage, processing, transport, distribution and marketing facilities, legislative and administrative policies and machinery affecting food, availability of inputs (including seeds and fertilizers), infrastructure (including irrigation networks and roads), technology, research, training and manpower in the food sector, and the ability to meet food emergencies. It then works out a plan to improve its food situation, so that enough food of sufficient nutritional value reaches all the people in the country. The aim of the food strategies is to build a greater degree of food self-reliance in countries where the need is greatest and to assure that the peoples' consumption needs are addressed.

In Africa alone, some 30 countries, with a total population approaching 500 million, have decided to adopt food strategies, and most have requested assistance from WFC for their preparation. Official development assistance from donor countries, needed to support the food strategies and programmes of developing countries in the period 1982-1987, has been estimated at more than $10 billion a year.

In addition to its efforts to increase food production in developing countries, WFC seeks to promote the establishment of an effective system of world food security through more open trade and assurances of continuity of food supplies for developing countries, as well as reserve programmes in support of a larger measure of food self-sufficiency.

Other United Nations programmes concerned with food aid include the **World Food Programme (WFP)**—which the United Nations sponsors jointly with the Food and Agriculture Organization of the United Nations—and the International Fund for Agricultural Development.

Population assistance

The United Nations has been concerned with population questions since its earliest years. The 27-member *Population Commission* was set up in 1947 as one of the functional commissions of the Economic and Social Council to arrange for studies and advise the Council on: the size and structure of populations and changes therein, and policies which influence them; the interplay of demographic on economic and social factors; and other demographic questions on which the United Nations and related agencies might seek advice. The Commission is supported by the *Population Division of the Department of Economic and Social Affairs*, which carries out studies requested by the Commission.

In addition, the Commission monitors population trends and policies, reviews and appraises progress towards achieving the goals of the World Population Plan of Action adopted at the World Population Conference (Bucharest, Romania) in 1974 (designated as *World Population Year*). It also follows up on the recommendations of the International Conference on Population (Mexico City, 1984).

The 1974 Action Plan had stressed the fundamental relationship between population factors and overall economic and social development. The 1984 Conference affirmed the Plan's validity, appraised progress during the decade and approved an updated global population strategy—in the form of 88 recommendations identifying areas where further action was needed and including the Mexico City Declaration on Population and Development containing principles underlying the recommendations. Target mortality rates were adjusted, and emerging issues, such as migration, urbanization, computerized data-processing and aging populations were addressed, as was the need for an intersectoral approach to population and development, for policies that respect individual and family rights and for improvement in the status of women and increasing their participation in all aspects of development.

The early work of the United Nations on population questions concentrated on the improvement of demographic statistics, which were lacking for large parts of the world, and then began to focus on the application of statistical data in analytical studies and in the preparation of world-wide population estimates and projections. The first *Demographic Yearbook* was published by the United Nations Statistical Office in 1948.

In the 1960s, the extraordinarily rapid rate at which the world's population was growing became an urgent concern (between 1950 and 1960, world population increased from 2.5 billion to over 3 billion, and it was projected to more than double by the year 2000; despite a recent decline in the global growth rate, it passed the 5 billion mark in mid-1987).

In 1966, the General Assembly authorized the United Nations to provide technical assistance in the population field and, the following year, it established a Trust Fund for Population Activities, renamed in 1969 the **United Nations Fund for Population Activities (UNFPA)**, to provide additional resources to the United Nations system for technical co-operation activities in the population field. In 1972, the UNDP Governing Council was designated as the Fund's governing body.

UNFPA is now the largest internationally funded source of assistance to population programmes in developing countries. The major portion of its funds, almost all of which come from voluntary governmental contributions, has been allocated to family-planning projects.

UNFPA's role is to build up the capacity to respond to needs in population and family planning, to promote understanding of population factors (population growth, fertility, mortality, spatial distribution and migration), to assist Governments to develop population goals and programmes, and to provide financial assistance to implement them. Its areas of work include family planning, communication and education, data collection and analysis, formulation and implementation of policies and programmes, special programmes (for women, youth, the aged, the handicapped, etc.) and activities such as conferences, documentation centres, clearing-houses and training.

Assistance to children

The *United Nations International Children's Emergency Fund* (UNICEF) was created by the General Assembly during its first session, in 1946, to meet the emergency needs of children in post-war Europe and China for food, drugs and clothing. In 1950, the Assembly changed the main emphasis of the Fund's mandate to programmes of long-range benefit to children of developing countries. Three years later, the Assembly decided that UNICEF should continue this work indefinitely. Its name was changed to the **United Nations Children's Fund**, but the well-known acronym "UNICEF" was retained.

Combining humanitarian and development objectives, UNICEF co-operates with developing countries in their efforts to protect their children and to enable them to develop their full potential. This co-operation takes place within the context of national development efforts and has as its goal the realization for every child of the opportunity to enjoy the basic rights and privileges embodied in the *Declaration of the Rights of the Child*, adopted by the General Assembly in 1959 (*see also* Other human rights questions *in* Chapter IV), and to contribute to their country's progress and well-being.

UNICEF co-operates with developing countries in several ways:

✧ it assists in the planning and extension of services benefiting children, in consultation with the countries concerned, and in the exchange of experience between countries;

✧ it provides funds to strengthen the training and orientation of national personnel, including health and sanitation workers, teachers, nutritionists and child-welfare specialists; and

✧ it delivers technical supplies, equipment and other aids, ranging from paper for textbooks to equipment and medicines for health clinics to pipes and pumps bringing clean water to villages.

Under its Basic Services strategy, adopted in 1976, UNICEF assists Governments to plan, develop and extend—in both rural and urban environments—low-cost community-based services in the interrelated fields of maternal and child health, applied nutrition, clean water and sanitation, formal and non-formal education, responsible parenthood and supporting services for women and girls.

Particular progress has been made in recent years in a UNICEF programme to bring about a virtual revolution in child survival and child development at low cost and in a relatively short time, emphasizing immunization, breast-feeding, growth monitoring and a simple oral rehydration method. A current major goal is universal child immunization against vaccine-preventable diseases by 1990 (*see also* World Health Organization *in* Chapter VII).

While UNICEF assistance is directed primarily towards long-range programmes for children, it moves swiftly to meet the immediate needs of children and mothers in emergencies arising from natural disasters, civil strife or epidemics. Emergency relief is followed by

UNICEF depends entirely on voluntary contributions to finance its activities. Nearly three quarters of its income derives from Governments; the rest comes from organizations and individuals, through greeting-card sales and various fund-raising campaigns.

UNICEF served as the "lead agency" in the United Nations system for the *International Year of the Child* (1979) and continues to be responsible for co-ordinating the follow-up activities of the Year related to the goals concerning children set forth in the International Development Strategy for the Third United Nations Development Decade.

UNICEF was awarded the Nobel Peace Prize in 1965.

* * * *

The protection of children was the subject of a declaration drawn up by the Commission for Social Development and adopted by the General Assembly in 1986. The *Declaration on Social and Legal Principles relating to the Protection and Welfare of Children, with Special Reference to Foster Placement and Adoption Nationally and Internationally* sought to reconcile various juridical principles on foster placement and adoption with religious laws and practices.

The role of women in development

International recognition of the important role that women play and should continue to play in the development process and of the need to intensify action to improve their condition was given prominence in 1975, proclaimed by the General Assembly as *International Women's Year*, focusing on the threefold objective of equality, development and peace.

Recognition of women's role in development culminated in the incorporation into the International Development Strategy for the Third United Nations Development Decade (1980s), of special provisions aimed at securing women's equal participation, both as agents and as beneficiaries, in the economic, social, political and cultural fields at the national, regional and international levels.

The highlight of International Women's Year was the convening in Mexico City of the first intergovernmental conference on women. The World Conference of the International Women's Year adopted the Declaration of Mexico on the Equality of Women and Their Contribution to Development and Peace, and a World Plan of Action for the implementation of the objectives of the International Women's Year.

Minimum objectives of the World Plan of Action included: a marked increase in literacy and civic education of women; extension of co-educational training in industry and agriculture; equal access to education; increased employment opportunities and reduction of unemployment and discrimination in the terms and conditions of employment; equal eligibility to vote and seek elected office; greater participation in policy-making positions; increased welfare services; parity of civil, social and political rights; and recognition of the value of women's work in the home and in other non-remunerated activities.

Later in 1975, the General Assembly endorsed the proposals of the Mexico Conference and proclaimed the period 1976-1985 as the *United Nations Decade for Women: Equality, Development and Peace*, to be devoted to implementing the World Plan of Action. At the same time, the Assembly established a *Voluntary Fund for the Decade* (whose activities, it was subsequently decided, would continue beyond the Decade through a separate *United Nations Development Fund for Women* in autonomous association with the United Nations Development Programme), and also approved the creation of the International Research and Training Institute for the Advancement of Women *(see under* Training and research *below).*

Convened at the mid-term of the Decade to evaluate progress, the World Conference of the United Nations Decade for Women: Equality, Development and Peace (Copenhagen, 1980) adopted a Programme of Action for the second half of the Decade, delineating specific action to promote the threefold objective of the Decade, with special emphasis on the subtheme: employment, health and education.

On the recommendation of the Conference, the General Assembly convened, at the conclusion of the Decade, a World Conference to Review and Appraise the Achievements of the United Nations Decade for Women (Nairobi, 1985). The Conference adopted Forward-looking Strategies for the Advancement of Women to the year 2000, a document detailing obstacles still to be overcome to achieve the Decade's goals, and setting forth basic strategies to be employed and measures to serve as guidelines, within national priorities, for implementing those strategies. In addition, emerging areas of concern were addressed, such as the economic value of underpaid work of women and their greater participation in decision-making, violence against women, data banks on women's issues, and family planning. The document also identified particularly vulnerable groups of women in need of special considerations.

In 1982, the General Assembly adopted a *Declaration on the Participation of Women in Promoting International Peace and Co-operation*, which states that special national and international measures are necessary to increase the level of women's participation in international relations so that women can contribute, on an equal basis with men, to national and international efforts to secure world peace and economic and social progress and to promote international co-operation.

See also Women's rights *in* Chapter IV.

Youth and development

By adopting, in 1965, the *Declaration on the Promotion among Youth of the Ideals of Peace, Mutual Respect and Understanding between Peoples*, the General Assembly stressed the importance of the role of youth in today's world, especially its potential contribution to development, and proposed that Governments give youth an opportunity to take part in preparing and carrying out national development plans and international co-operation programmes.

Accordingly, activities of the United Nations and its Member States have focused on: the preparation of youth, through education, for full participation in all aspects of life and development; health policies and programmes which would ensure that young people are able to take advantage of opportunities open to them; the adoption of all possible means to increase employment for youth; opening up channels of communication between the United Nations and youth organizations; and promoting human rights and their enjoyment by youth.

The *World Youth Assembly* (Headquarters, July 1970) was the first such meeting organized by the United Nations.

The General Assembly decided, in 1979, to proclaim 1985 as *International Youth Year: Participation, Development and Peace*, aimed at bringing about widespread awareness of the situation of youth, their problems and aspirations, with a view to engaging young people in the development process. The Specific Programme of Measures and Activities adopted by the Assembly in 1981, together with regional and national plans of action, became the instruments of observance for the International Youth Year.

The symbolic culmination of the Year came in the form of a series of plenary meetings of the General Assembly at its 1985 session, in November, designated as the United Nations World Conference for the International Youth Year. The outcome of the Conference was the adoption of guidelines for further planning and suitable follow-up in the field of youth, encompassing all the experience gathered during the preparations for the Year and representing an international instrument providing contours of a global strategy for youth work beyond the Year. In recognition of the importance of the guidelines as a conceptual framework in developing national youth policies and programmes, the Assembly and the Economic and Social Council have adopted several resolutions calling for their implementation by Governments and intergovernmental and non-governmental organizations at all levels.

A trust fund established for International Youth Year, renamed the *United Nations Youth Fund*, has continued to operate since 1985 to support projects of a catalytic or replicable nature involving young people in the development of their countries.

Aging and the elderly

The question of the elderly was first discussed by the General Assembly in 1948. In recent years, the needs of older persons, a rapidly growing sector of the world's population, and the impact of aging on development have received increasing attention in the United Nations.

In 1973, the Assembly considered a comprehensive report on the question of aging and, in 1978, decided to convene a World Assembly on Aging (Vienna, 1982). The World Assembly adopted an International Plan of Action on Aging, which emphasized the need for policies and plans to help the elderly as individuals and to deal with the long-term social and economic effects of aging populations. Recommendations in the Plan of Action cover: the need to help the elderly lead independent lives in their own family and community; giving them a choice as to the kind of health care they receive, and the importance of preventive care; providing support services to help families, particularly low-income families, to care for elderly relatives; and providing social security schemes, employment and adequate housing. The Plan of Action also includes recommendations for meeting the needs of particularly vulnerable groups, such as elderly refugees and migrant workers.

The *Commission for Social Development*, which has been entrusted with reviewing implementation of the Plan every four years, first reviewed it in 1985, taking into account a report indicating that by the year 2025, more than 70 per cent of persons over 60 would live in developing countries. The Commission identified priorities for action, such as creation of national committees on aging, co-ordinated planning, and strengthening of information exchange, training, research and education programmes. The General Assembly and the Economic and Social Council, in several resolutions, have urged Governments and non-governmental organizations to give priority in their activities to the question of aging.

The *United Nations Trust Fund for Aging* assists developing countries, at their request, in activities aimed at formulating and implementing policies and programmes on aging.

Disabled persons

In 1971, the General Assembly adopted the *Declaration on the Rights of Mentally Retarded Persons*, which states that such individuals have, to the maximum degree of feasibility, the same rights as other human beings, including the rights to medical care, to economic security and to live with his or her own family or with foster parents. In cases where the rights of mentally retarded persons may have to be restricted or denied, the Assembly declared that there must be legal safeguards against any form of abuse.

The *Declaration on the Rights of Disabled Persons*, adopted by the Assembly in 1975, proclaims that disabled persons have the same civil and political rights as other human beings. It sets out the right of disabled persons to treatment and services that would develop their capabilities to the maximum and hasten their social integration or reintegration. Other provisions include their right to economic and social security and to employment or a useful and remunerative occupation.

When in 1976 the General Assembly decided to proclaim 1981 *International Year of Disabled Persons*, it called for a plan of action for the Year at the national, regional and international levels, with the emphasis on primary health care, rehabilitation and prevention of disability. The Year's purpose, and its theme, was the promotion of "full participation and equality", defined as the right of disabled persons to take part fully in the life and development of their societies, to enjoy living conditions equal to those of other citizens and to have an equal share in improved conditions resulting from socio-economic development. Other objectives included increasing public understanding of disability and encouraging disabled persons to organize themselves to express their views effectively.

The Year's activities were followed by the Assembly's adoption, in 1982, of a World Programme of Action concerning Disabled Persons, aimed at continuing long-term programmes at the national, regional and international levels, and by its proclamation of the *United Nations Decade of Disabled Persons* (1983-1992), encouraging Member States to utilize this period to carry out the Programme.

The United Nations Trust Fund for the International Year of Disabled Persons was renamed in 1985 the *Voluntary Fund for the United Nations Decade of Disabled Persons*, to be continued throughout the Decade to help meet requests for assistance from developing countries and organizations of disabled persons to further the implementation of the Programme.

Refugees

According to the Statute of the **Office of the United Nations High Commissioner for Refugees (UNHCR)**, a refugee is a person who, owing to a well-founded fear of persecution for reasons of race, religion, nationality, membership of a particular social group or political opinion, is outside the country of his nationality and is unable or, owing to such fear, unwilling to avail himself of the protection of that country.

The essential problems of refugees, and the necessary solutions to them, have been the same throughout history and around the world: refugees need to be fed, clothed and sheltered; they want to go back home if they can, and often need help to do so; and they need to find new homes if they cannot return to their old ones;

The Office of the United Nations High Commissioner for Refugees was established by the General Assembly in 1950 to protect refugees and promote durable solutions to their problems. UNHCR depends entirely on voluntary contributions from Governments and private sources for its programmes, seeking to assist as many as possible of the more than 12 million refugees in the world.

The basic function of UNHCR is to extend international protection to refugees who, by definition, do not enjoy the protection of their former home country. UNHCR seeks to ensure that refugees receive asylum and are granted a favourable legal status in their asylum country. An essential element of this legal status is the safeguard provided by the generally accepted principle of *non-refoulement*, which prohibits expulsion or forcible return of a person to a country where he may have reason to fear persecution. UNHCR also seeks to ensure that persons claiming to be refugees are identified as such so as to enable them to take advantage of the standards set forth in international instruments or under international law.

The legal status of refugees has been defined more specifically in two international instruments—the 1951 *Convention relating to the Status of Refugees* and its 1967 Protocol—which define the rights and duties of refugees and contain provisions dealing with such matters as protection from *refoulement*, unlawful expulsions and detentions, and the refugee's employment, public education and assistance, artistic rights and industrial property. In regard to many of these matters, refugees are to receive the same treatment as nationals of their country of residence.

Material assistance is also essential, to enable refugees or displaced persons to achieve permanent solutions to their problems, whether it be through voluntary repatriation, local settlement in the country of first asylum or migration to another country. Measures vary widely according to need. Integration through rural settlement is in general the best solution for refugees of rural background who cannot hope to repatriate for some time; in Africa, in particular, UNHCR helps refugees to settle on the land through the establishment of new rural communities or through strengthening the infrastructure of areas where the refugees can be absorbed spontaneously into the local population.

Assistance in voluntary repatriation may involve a large-scale transportation and settlement operation, or may simply entail the payment of travel expenses for individuals.

Resettlement of Latin American and Indo-Chinese refugees are examples of instances where UNHCR's role has been to negotiate with Governments to encourage the admission of refugees or displaced persons into their territories.

UNHCR has for many years helped to organize special resettlement schemes for refugees who could not qualify under normal immigration criteria because of physical or social handicaps. In addition, family reunion is an essential activity, and counselling plays an important role in helping individual refugees find the most appropriate solutions to their problems.

UNHCR was awarded the Nobel Peace Prize in 1954 and in 1981.

The Second International Conference for Assistance to Refugees in Africa (ICARA II) was held at Geneva in July 1984. It adopted a Declaration and Programme of Action aimed at initiating a long-term strategy to deal with Africa's 4 million refugees and returnees. Going beyond the first International Conference (ICARA I) (Geneva, 1981), which focused primarily on emergency assistance, ICARA II linked humanitarian aid to refugees with the need to help host countries develop their social and economic infrastructures.

See also United Nations Relief and Works Agency for Palestine Refugees in the Near East *in section on the* Middle East *in* Chapter II.)

Disaster relief and special economic assistance

Following a series of major disasters in the late 1960s, the need for further support of world-wide emergency relief assistance, which had been provided for many years by individual Governments, United Nations agencies, the Red Cross and other voluntary agencies, became increasingly apparent.

In 1971, the General Assembly decided to establish a central office within the United Nations to mobilize relief more rapidly, co-ordinate it more systematically and reduce risks of waste or duplication of effort or of failure to supply essential items. It was also recognized that more could and should be done to improve contingency planning and preparedness and to harness modern scientific and technological knowledge to prevent disasters and mitigate their effects.

The **Office of the United Nations Disaster Relief Co-ordinator (UNDRO),** with headquarters in Geneva, began operations in March 1972. In this way, it acts as a focal point and clearing-house for information on relief needs and on what donors are sending to meet those needs. UNDRO mobilizes and co-ordinates the relief assistance of the various organizations of the United Nations system and co-ordinates that assistance with what is given by others. UNDRO's functions include:

♦ gathering information from many sources on individual disaster situations and disseminating it to Governments and other potential donors of aid;

♦ organizing missions to assess needs arising from natural disasters and other disaster situations;

♦ contacting potential donors, mobilizing relief contributions and ensuring the rapid transport of relief supplies; and

♦ during the post-emergency phase, advising Governments on disaster-prevention concepts in rehabilitation or reconstruction programmes and on the improvement of disaster preparedness planning generally.

UNDRO also promotes the study, prevention, control and prediction of natural disasters and provides Governments that request it with assistance in pre-disaster planning.

The United Nations also provides special assistance to individual countries afflicted by civil strife or other man-made disasters, facing severe economic and financial difficulties and/or requiring aid for reconstruction, rehabilitation and development. Many of these countries are among the least-developed in the world and some are also geographically handicapped—that is, land-locked or island countries.

The Sudano-Sahelian region of Africa, afflicted since the 1960s with a prolonged drought, accelerating desertification and other disasters compounding an already serious economic situation straining fragile economies, provides an example of United Nations disaster relief coupled with long-range assistance. The **United Nations Sudano-Sahelian Office (UNSO)** was established in 1973 to assist in medium- and long-term rehabilitation and development programmes of the Sahel's eight drought-stricken countries—Burkina Faso, Cape Verde, Chad, Gambia, Mali, Mauritania, Niger and Senegal, members of the Permanent Inter-State Committee for Drought Control in the Sahel (known as CILSS from its French acronym). Five years later, UNSO's mandate was expanded to cover 14 additional African countries—Benin, Cameroon, Djibouti, Ethiopia, Ghana, Guinea, Guinea-Bissau, Kenya, Nigeria, Somalia, Sudan, Togo, Uganda and United Republic of Tanzania—and the implementation of the Plan of Action to Combat Desertification *(see* Protection of the environment *above)*. Six of these countries—Djibouti, Ethiopia, Kenya, Somalia, Sudan, Uganda—are members of the Intergovernmental Authority for Drought and Development (IGADD), created by them in January 1986. Projects are financed in part by the *United Nations Fund for Sudano-Sahelian Activities*.

Focusing concerted attention on the worsening plight of African countries, the General Assembly in December 1984 adopted a Declaration on the Critical Economic Situation in Africa, which constituted a framework for concerted action by the international community. Effective 1 January 1985, the Secretary-General established a United Nations Office for Emergency Operations in Africa which, until it was phased out in October 1986, co-ordinated and provided assistance to help ensure a broad yet concentrated international response to the continuing drought-related crisis in sub-Saharan Africa.

In March 1985, the Secretary-General convened, at Geneva, an International Conference on the Emergency Situation in Africa, followed by consultations on the emergency needs of individual countries, in order to direct the general commitments made at the Conference to specific country needs.

In June 1986, at the close of its first special session devoted to the economic problems of a single region, the General Assembly adopted the United Nations Programme of Action for African Economic Recovery and Development, 1986-1990, whereby the international community committed its support for initiatives being undertaken by African States to promote food production, build up agricultural industries and related infrastructure, reverse the effects of drought and desertification, and develop human resources. The African States themselves expected to provide two thirds of the estimated $120 billion required, and hoped that the international community would make available the remainder.

International control of narcotic drugs and psychotropic substances

Control of narcotic drugs has been a world concern ever since the first international conference on the subject was held in Shanghai in 1909. The international control system has been built up step by step, beginning in 1920 under the auspices of the League of Nations and since 1946 by the United Nations.

A series of treaties adopted under the auspices of the United Nations require that Governments exercise control over production and distribution of narcotic drugs and psychotropic substances, combat illicit traffic, maintain the necessary administrative machinery and report to international organs on their actions. This international régime includes:

✧ the *Single Convention on Narcotic Drugs*, 1961 (in force since 1964), which consolidates earlier treaties on natural or synthetic narcotics, cannabis and cocaine;

✧ the *Convention on Psychotropic Substances*, 1971 (in force since 1976), which covers hallucinogens, amphetamines, barbiturates, non-barbiturate sedatives and tranquillizers; and

✧ the 1972 *Protocol amending the Single Convention* (in force since 1975), which highlights the need for treatment and rehabilitation of drug addicts.

The central objective of these treaties is to limit the supply of and demand for narcotic drugs and psychotropic substances to medical and scientific needs. The *Commission on Narcotic Drugs*, one of the functional commissions of the Economic and Social Council, considers all matters pertaining to the aims and implementation of the treaties, and makes recommendations to the Council on the control of narcotic drugs and psychotropic substances. The Commission is thus the main policy-making body for international drug control within the United Nations system and has primary responsibility for amending the schedules annexed to the international treaties in order to bring substances under international control, delete them from control or change the régime of control to which they are subject. The *Division of Narcotic Drugs* acts as the secretariat to the Commission and also carries out various functions entrusted to the Secretary-General under the international drug control treaties.

The *International Narcotics Control Board*, which began operating in 1968, is responsible for the continuous evaluation and overall supervision of governmental implementation of drug control treaties. It reviews and confirms annual estimates of licit narcotic drug requirements submitted by Governments which limit the manufacture and trade in narcotic drugs to medical and scientific purposes, and also monitors the licit movement of psychotropic substances. It may, in cases of breaches of the treaties, require Governments to adopt remedial measures, and it may bring treaty violations to the attention of the parties, the Economic and Social Council and the Commission on Narcotic Drugs.

The *United Nations Fund for Drug Abuse Control*, established in 1971, assists Governments, at their request, by helping finance projects aimed at reducing the illicit supply of and demand for drugs— for example, projects to replace illicit opium poppy cultivation, treat and rehabilitate drug addicts, strengthen control measures and organize information and education programmes. The Fund relies entirely on voluntary contributions.

In 1981, the General Assembly, called for an international campaign against traffic in drugs, adopted an International Drug Abuse Control Strategy and a five-year programme which called for integrated action at the national, regional and international levels, co-ordinated through the United Nations.

In 1984, the Assembly adopted a *Declaration on the Control of Drug Trafficking and Drug Abuse*, calling for intensified efforts and co-ordinated strategies aimed at the control and eradication of those complex problems. Shortly thereafter, work began on preparing a convention against illicit traffic in narcotic drugs and psychotropic substances, addressing areas not covered by existing treaties.

Based on the premise that, with respect to the drug problem, both demand and supply have to be addressed if the problem is to be

attenuated, the first International Conference on Drug Abuse and Illicit Trafficking was held at Vienna in June 1987. The principal document adopted by the Conference was a Comprehensive Multidisciplinary Outline of Future Activities relevant to the Problems of Drug
Abuse and Illicit Trafficking. It contained recommendations for practical action to be taken by Governments and organizations to prevent
and reduce demand for narcotic drugs and psychotropic substances,
control supply, suppress illicit trafficking, and promote policies for
effective treatment and rehabilitation. A Declaration committed the
participants to take vigorous international action against drug abuse
and illicit trafficking. It also expressed the determination of participants
to strengthen action and co-operation at the national, regional and
interregional levels towards the goal of a society free of drug abuse.

Prevention of crime and treatment of offenders

United Nations work in the field of crime prevention and criminal justice has two main purposes: to lessen the human and material
costs of crime and its impact on socio-economic development, and
to promote the observance of international standards and norms in
criminal justice. To this end, the United Nations furthers the dissemination and exchange of information, the training of personnel and direct
aid to Governments at their request.

To provide a forum for the presentation of policies and to stimulate progress, the General Assembly in 1950 authorized the convening every five years of a *United Nations Congress on the Prevention
of Crime and the Treatment of Offenders*. Participants in the congresses include criminologists, penologists and senior police officers,
as well as experts in criminal law, human rights and rehabilitation.
Six such congresses have been held:

 ✧ the First Congress (Geneva, 1955) approved a set of
Standard Minimum Rules for the Treatment of Prisoners,
which the Economic and Social Council adopted in 1957;

 ✧ the Second Congress (London, 1960) dealt with measures for preventing juvenile delinquency and considered the
questions of prison labour, parole and after-care;

 ✧ the Third Congress (Stockholm, 1965) approved measures for crime prevention action by the community and for
combating recidivism;

 ✧ the Fourth Congress (Tokyo, 1970) stressed the need to
take crime into account in development planning, particularly

in view of the effects of urbanization, industrialization and the technological revolution on the human environment;

⬥ the Fifth Congress (Geneva, 1975) adopted the *Declaration on the Protection of All Persons from Torture and Other Cruel, Inhuman and Degrading Treatment or Punishment*, which the General Assembly approved later the same year (*see also* The fight against torture *in* Chapter IV); it also laid the basis for the *Code of Conduct for Law Enforcement Officials*, which was approved by the Assembly in 1979;

⬥ the Sixth Congress (Caracas, 1980) dealt with such topics as crime trends and crime prevention strategies, juvenile delinquency, crime and the abuse of power, and deinstitutionalization of corrections; the Caracas Declaration was endorsed later in 1980 by the General Assembly;

⬥ the Seventh Congress (Milan, 1985) adopted the Milan Plan of Action for strengthening international co-operation in crime prevention and criminal justice, which was subsequently approved by the General Assembly. Among other Congress documents (on which the Assembly took action in 1985) were: a set of Guiding Principles for Crime Prevention and Criminal Justice in the Context of Development and a New International Economic Order (endorsed); Basic Principles on the Independence of the Judiciary (endorsed); a Model Agreement on the Transfer of Foreign Prisoners (endorsed); a *Declaration on Basic Principles of Justice for Victims of Crime and Abuse of Power* (adopted); and *Standard Minimum Rules for the Administration of Juvenile Justice*, known as the Beijing Rules (adopted).

The Economic and Social Council's *Committee on Crime Prevention and Control* acts as preparatory body for the Congresses. It also advises the Secretary-General, the Commission for Social Development and, where appropriate, other United Nations organs, in formulating programmes for international action in its field of expertise, and recommends appropriate measures in law enforcement, judicial procedures and correctional practices.

United Nations research and training activities in the field of crime prevention and control are furthered by the *United Nations Social Defence Research Institute*, headquartered in Rome, and by regional training and research institutes in Africa, Asia and the Far East, Latin America, the Arab States and Europe.

The *United Nations Trust Fund for Social Defence* facilitates technical co-operation and exchange of information and experience in the field of crime prevention and control.

Training and research

Following a 1963 decision of the General Assembly, the **United Nations Institute for Training and Research (UNITAR)** was established in 1965 as an autonomous body within the framework of the United Nations. Its purpose is to enhance the effectiveness of the United Nations in achieving the major objectives of the Organization, particularly the maintenance of international peace and security and the promotion of economic and social development. UNITAR is supported by voluntary contributions from Member States, intergovernmental organizations, private foundations and other sources.

The Institute's training programmes deal with subjects of practical value to members of permanent missions to the United Nations. They include orientation courses on the United Nations, courses on international economics, workshops on drafting and negotiation of international legal instruments, on dispute settlement and on United Nations documentation, as well as issue-oriented training on peace, security, human rights and humanitarian assistance. The Institute, in co-operation with the United Nations, also organizes a fellowship programme and regional refresher courses in international law. Special courses and advisory services to diplomatic institutes of developing countries are also offered at the request of Member States; training courses in multilateral diplomacy and international co-operation for diplomats and government officials are financed through special-purpose grants.

Research activities aim at improving United Nations efficacy in analysing policy options, anticipating problems and launching new activities; others relate to the impact of the system on the private sector, building up the institutional memory of the Organization and studying issues not covered elsewhere in the system.

In addition, research includes work on devising a global model of economic development, a series of studies on alternative development strategies for the future of developing regions, and studies on the supply aspects of energy and natural resources. A series of conferences on different aspects of energy supplies have been held since 1976.

UNITAR was restructured by the General Assembly as from 1 January 1987. Training was to be the main focus of activities during an interim period until measures could be taken to provide UNITAR with financing on a more predictable, assured and continuous basis.

* * * *

The **United Nations Institute for Disarmament Research (UNIDIR),** set up provisionally in 1980 within the framework of UNITAR, has issued a number of research papers on aspects of arms control and disarmament. In 1982, the General Assembly decided to establish UNIDIR as an autonomous institute of the United Nations to undertake independent research on disarmament and related problems, particularly international security issues, and approved its Statute in 1984. Voluntary contributions from States and public and private organizations form the principal financing for UNIDIR's activities.

* * * *

The idea for the establishment of a United Nations university, international in character and devoted to the United Nations Charter objectives of peace and progress, was first put forward in 1969 by Secretary-General U Thant. In 1973, the General Assembly approved the Charter of the **United Nations University (UNU),** with its headquarters in Tokyo, under the joint sponsorship of the United Nations and the United Nations Educational, Scientific and Cultural Organization. UNU began operations in September 1975 as an autonomous institution within the framework of the United Nations.

Unlike traditional universities, UNU has no students of its own, no faculty, no campus. It is, rather, an international community of scholars engaged in research, post-graduate training and the dissemination of knowledge to help solve pressing global problems of human survival, development and welfare. It operates through world-wide networks of academic and research institutions and individual scholars concerned with nine programme areas: peace and conflict resolution; the global economy; energy systems and policy; resource policy and management; the food-energy nexus; food, nutrition, biotechnology and poverty; human and social development; regional perspectives; and science, technology and the information society.

UNU has established two research and training centres: one for development economics research, in Finland, and one for natural resources in Africa, in Côte d'Ivoire.

* * * *

Created in 1963 as an autonomous United Nations activity, the **United Nations Research Institute for Social Development (UNRISD)** conducts research into problems and policies of social development, based on two themes: improving the livelihood of the world's poor and increasing their participation in development.

The Institute's research programmes, usually carried out in collaboration with national research institutions, focus on the socio-economic dimensions of development problems. Work priorities include study of food security for all, the social situation of refugees, measurement and analysis of social and economic development, the social impact of adjustment policies, and the social impact of urbanization.

The Institute, which has its headquarters at Geneva, is financed entirely by voluntary contributions.

*   *   *   *

On the recommendation of the 1975 World Conference of the International Women's Year, the General Assembly established the **International Research and Training Institute for the Advancement of Women (INSTRAW)**, endorsing its Statute in 1985. The Institute is an autonomous body within the United Nations system with a mandate to carry out research, training and information activities worldwide to promote women as key agents of development. To extend its outreach, INSTRAW works in close co-operation with the United Nations and governmental and non-governmental organizations, and has developed a growing network of focal points and correspondents.

The Institute is funded by voluntary contributions from United Nations Member States, inter- and non-governmental organizations, foundations and private sources. It began operations in 1979, and has its headquarters in Santo Domingo, Dominican Republic. Through the close interlinkage of its research, training and information activities, INSTRAW addresses the practical aspects of rethinking development and the place of women in this process.

CHAPTER IV

The United Nations at work for human rights

As stated in the preamble to the Organization's Charter, the peoples of the United Nations declare their determination "to promote social progress and better standards of life in larger freedom". It is thus that Article 1 of the Charter proclaims that one of the purposes of the United Nations is to achieve international co-operation in promoting and encouraging respect for human rights and fundamental freedoms for all without distinction as to race, sex, language or religion.

Universal Declaration of Human Rights

One of the first major achievements of the United Nations was the adoption by the General Assembly, on 10 December 1948, of the Universal Declaration of Human Rights. The Assembly proclaimed the Declaration as "a common standard of achievement for all peoples and all nations", and it called upon all Member States and all peoples to promote and secure the effective recognition and observance of the rights and freedoms set forth in the Declaration.

In 1950, the General Assembly decided that 10 December of each year should be observed as *Human Rights Day* all over the world.

Articles 1 and 2 of the Declaration state that "all human beings are born free and equal in dignity and rights" and are entitled to all the rights and freedoms set forth in the Declaration, "without distinction of any kind, such as race, colour, sex, language, religion, political or other opinion, national or social origin, property, birth or other status".

Articles 3 to 21 of the Declaration set forth the civil and political rights to which all human beings are entitled, including:

  ✧ the right to life, liberty and security of person;

  ✧ freedom from slavery and servitude;

  ✧ freedom from torture or cruel, inhuman or degrading treatment or punishment;

✧ the right to recognition as a person before the law; equal protection of the law; the right to an effective judicial remedy; freedom from arbitrary arrest, detention or exile; the right to a fair trial and public hearing by an independent and impartial tribunal; the right to be presumed innocent until proved guilty;

✧ freedom from arbitrary interference with privacy, family, home or correspondence;

✧ freedom of movement; the right of asylum; the right to a nationality;

✧ the right to marry and to found a family; the right to own property;

✧ freedom of thought, conscience and religion; freedom of opinion and expression;

✧ the right of association and of assembly;

✧ the right to take part in government and the right of equal access to public service.

Articles 22 to 27 of the Declaration set forth the economic, social and cultural rights to which all human beings are entitled, including:

✧ the right to social security;

✧ the right to work; the right to rest and leisure;

✧ the right to a standard of living adequate for health and well-being;

✧ the right to education;

✧ the right to participate in the cultural life of the community.

The concluding articles—28 to 30—recognize that everyone is entitled to a social and international order in which these rights and freedoms may be fully realized, and they stress the duties and responsibilities which the individual owes to the community.

International Covenants on Human Rights

Following the adoption of the Universal Declaration of Human Rights, work began on the drafting of two International Covenants on Human Rights—one on economic, social and cultural rights and the other on civil and political rights—to put into binding legal form the rights proclaimed in the Declaration.

The International Covenant on Economic, Social and Cultural Rights, the International Covenant on Civil and Political Rights and the Optional Protocol to the latter Covenant were adopted unanimously by the General Assembly on 16 December 1966.

Although the Covenants are based on the Universal Declaration of Human Rights, the rights covered are not identical. The most important right regulated in both Covenants and not contained in the Declaration is the right of peoples to self-determination, including the right of peoples freely to dispose of their natural wealth and resources.

The *International Covenant on Economic, Social and Cultural Rights* entered into force on 3 January 1976. By 30 June 1987, 90 States had ratified or acceded to it.

The Covenant deals with conditions of work, trade unions, social security, protection of the family, standards of living and health, education and cultural life. It provides for the progressive full realization of those rights without discrimination. States parties to the Covenant submit periodic reports to the Economic and Social Council. The *Committee on Economic, Social and Cultural Rights*, an 18-member body of independent experts set up by the Council to assist it in implementing the Covenant, studies the reports and discusses them with representatives of the Governments concerned. The Committee makes recommendations to the Council on helping States parties to put the Covenant's rights into effect.

The *International Covenant on Civil and Political Rights* and the *Optional Protocol* entered into force on 23 March 1976. By 30 June 1987, 86 States had ratified or acceded to the Covenant and 38 States had ratified or acceded to the Protocol.

The Covenant deals with such rights as freedom of movement, equality before the law, presumption of innocence, freedom of conscience and religion, freedom of opinion and expression, peaceful assembly, freedom of association, participation in public affairs and elections, and minority rights. It prohibits arbitrary deprivation of life; torture, cruel or degrading treatment or punishment; slavery and forced labour; arbitrary arrest or detention and arbitrary interference with privacy; war propaganda, and advocacy of racial or religious hatred that constitutes an incitement to discrimination or violence.

The Covenant established an 18-member *Human Rights Committee*, which considers reports submitted by States parties on measures taken to implement the Covenant's provisions, and also considers communications alleging violations under the Optional Protocol.

The *Optional Protocol to the International Covenant on Civil and Political Rights* provides for the consideration of communications from individuals who claim to be victims of violations of any rights set forth in the Covenant. Only claims against States parties to the Protocol can be considered.

Elimination of racial discrimination

In 1963, the General Assembly adopted the *United Nations Declaration on the Elimination of All Forms of Racial Discrimination*, which affirms that discrimination between human beings on the grounds of race, colour or ethnic origin is an offence to human dignity, a denial of Charter principles, a violation of the rights proclaimed in the Universal Declaration of Human Rights and an obstacle to friendly and peaceful relations among peoples.

Two years later, the Assembly adopted the *International Convention on the Elimination of All Forms of Racial Discrimination*. The Convention entered into force on 4 January 1969; by 30 June 1987, 124 States were party to it. It defines racial discrimination as "any distinction, exclusion, restriction or preference based on race, colour, descent or national or ethnic origin which has the purpose of effect of nullifying or impairing the recognition, enjoyment or exercise, on an equal footing, of human rights and fundamental freedoms in the political, economic, social, cultural or any other fields of public life". States parties undertake to pursue a policy of eliminating racial discrimination and promoting understanding among races.

The *Committee on the Elimination of Racial Discrimination*, an 18-member body of experts set up by the Convention, reviews reports submitted by States parties on the measures they have adopted to implement the Convention, discusses the reports with government representatives and makes general recommendations. It may also consider complaints submitted by individuals or groups alleging that the Convention has been violated, provided that the State concerned has made a declaration under article 14 of the Convention recognizing the competence of the Committee to receive such complaints.

In 1973, the General Assembly adopted the *International Convention on the Suppression and Punishment of the Crime of Apartheid*. The Convention, which entered into force on 18 July 1976, provides that international responsibility for the crime of *apartheid* shall apply to individuals, members of organizations and institutions, and representatives of a State, whether residing in the State in which the acts are perpetrated or elsewhere. Persons charged can be tried by any State party to the Convention. A three-member Group of the Commission on Human Rights meets each year to review progress in implementing the Convention. As of 30 June 1987, 85 States were parties to the Convention.

The Assembly also decided in 1973 to designate the 10-year period beginning on 10 December 1973 as the *Decade for Action to Combat Racism and Racial Discrimination*, and called on all States to work towards the goals of the Decade by: promoting human rights, especially by eradicating racism and racial discrimination; identifying and dispelling the fallacious beliefs that contribute to racism; arresting any expansion of racist policies; and putting an end to racist régimes.

The mid-point of the Decade was marked by a World Conference (Geneva, August 1978), which adopted a Programme of Action, including recommendations for comprehensive mandatory sanctions against the racist régimes of southern Africa, elimination by Governments of all discriminatory laws and practices, adoption of laws to punish dissemination of ideas based on racial superiority or hatred, and promotion of the rights of indigenous peoples and migrant workers.

In 1979, the Assembly adopted a programme for the remaining four years of the Decade, designed to accelerate progress towards the elimination of racial discrimination.

The Second World Conference to Combat Racism and Racial Discrimination (Geneva, 1983) found that, in spite of the efforts of the international community during the Decade, racial discrimination and *apartheid* showed no signs of diminishing. The Conference adopted a Declaration and a Programme of Action for a renewed effort to end racial discrimination and *apartheid*.

On the recommendation of the Conference, the General Assembly, on 22 November, proclaimed the 10-year period beginning on 10 December 1983 as the *Second Decade to Combat Racism and Racial Discrimination* and approved a Programme of Action for the Second Decade, including: action to combat *apartheid*; education, teaching and training; dissemination of information and the role of the mass media in combating racism and racial discrimination; action by non-governmental organizations; and international cooperation.

See also Apartheid *in* Chapter II.

The fight against torture

In 1975, the General Assembly adopted the *Declaration on the Protection of All Persons from Being Subjected to Torture and Other*

Cruel, Inhuman or Degrading Treatment or Punishment, which states that such acts are an offence to human dignity and a violation of human rights and fundamental freedoms. In 1982, it adopted the *Principles of Medical Ethics*, relating to the role of health personnel, particularly physicians, in the protection of prisoners and detainees against torture and other cruel, inhuman or degrading treatment or punishment.

The *Convention against Torture and Other Cruel, Inhuman or Degrading Treatment or Punishment*, adopted by the Assembly in 1984, entered into force on 26 June 1987. By 30 June 1987, there were 20 States parties to the Convention, which obliges States to make torture a crime and prosecute and punish those guilty of it; neither higher orders nor exceptional circumstances can justify torture. The Convention provides for the trial of torturers in the courts of States parties, no matter where the torture took place. It also allows, when the proper conditions are fulfilled, for investigation by an independent committee, which can also receive complaints from individuals against States that have accepted the Committee's power to do so.

Treatment and rehabilitation programmes for torture victims and their families are offered through the *United Nations Voluntary Fund for Victims of Torture*, which accepts contributions from Governments, organizations and individuals.

Complaints of violations of human rights

Individuals may complain to the United Nations of violations of their human rights under procedures provided for in the Optional Protocol to the International Covenant on Civil and Political Rights, the Convention on the Elimination of All Forms of Racial Discrimination and the Convention against Torture. In addition, another procedure exists for dealing with the thousands of letters and reports received each year but which fall outside those specific procedures.

Communications containing complaints of violations of human rights are summarized and sent confidentially to the 43-member *Commission on Human Rights*, a functional commission of the Economic and Social Council, and to its *Sub-Commission on Prevention of Discrimination and Protection of Minorities*, made up of 26 experts elected by the Commission. Copies of the complaint are also sent to the Member States named. The identity of the writers is not disclosed, unless they have consented to disclosure. Any replies from the Government are forwarded to the Commission and Sub-Commission.

The Sub-Commission, if it finds the communications appear to reveal "a consistent pattern of gross and reliably attested violations" of human rights, may refer the situation to the Commission which, in turn, can decide to carry out a thorough study of the situation or to name an *ad hoc* committee to investigate it. All these procedures are confidential and are dealt with in private meetings until a report, if any, is made by the Commission to the Economic and Social Council.

Putting an end to violations

The Commission on Human Rights and its Sub-Commission also consider in public session each year the question of violations of human rights and fundamental freedoms, including racial discrimination and *apartheid*, in various countries and territories, as well as other human rights situations. Governments and non-governmental organizations present information on violations and, often, the Governments criticized are there to present clarifications or reply. When situations are sufficiently serious, the Commission may decide to order an investigation by independent and objective experts and to call upon the Government concerned to bring about needed changes.

A number of specific situations have been dealt with, for example:

◇ *In southern Africa*. Since 1967, an *ad hoc* working group of experts of the Commission on Human Rights has reported regularly on allegations of ill-treatment of opponents of *apartheid* and other racist policies, on infringements of trade union rights and on the treatment of political prisoners and detainees, in South Africa and Namibia.

◇ *In the occupied Arab territories, including Palestine*: Since 1968, the Commission has been considering the question of the violation of human rights in the territories occupied by Israel as a result of the 1967 hostilities in the Middle East, including Israel's violation of the 1949 Geneva Convention relative to the Protection of Civilian Persons in Time of War.

◇ *Other situations*. In 1975, the Commission established a five-member Working Group to study the human rights situation in Chile. The Group visited Chile in 1978 and submitted a report to the General Assembly and the Commission. After the completion of the Group's mandate, the Commission, in 1979, appointed a special rapporteur to continue to study the situation. The Commission has requested that studies or reports be prepared by special rapporteurs or by the Secretary-General on the human rights situation in a number of other countries. Currently, reports are being prepared on the situation in Afghanistan, El Salvador and Iran. The situation in other countries is under review either in the Commission's public meetings or in the confidential procedure. The Commission has also named experts to assess, in co-operation with the Government concerned, the assistance needed to help restore full enjoyment of human rights.

The Commission studies human rights violations not only in specific countries but as global phenomena, i.e. particularly serious violations found to occur in many parts of the world. In this connection, the Commission, in 1980, set up a five-member *Working Group on Enforced or Involuntary Disappearances*, which receives reports of cases of disappearances from all over the world and transmits them on a humanitarian basis to the Governments concerned in order to help families find missing relatives.

Special rapporteurs have been named to investigate reports of summary or arbitrary executions wherever they occur, and to look into reports of torture. Both rapporteurs receive reports from individuals and organizations and deal with the Governments concerned in an attempt to clarify allegations and bring torture or summary or arbitrary executions to an end.

In the above instances, the United Nations can urgently intervene with Governments with regard to reported disappearances, torture or threatened executions when the minimum international standards of fair trial and appeal appear not to have been met. Such urgent appeals meet with positive responses in many cases and contribute to saving lives and protecting the physical integrity of individuals.

Women's rights

The *Commission on the Status of Women*, a functional commission of the Economic and Social Council established in 1946, prepares recommendations on promoting women's rights and on problems requiring attention in this field.

The General Assembly's first legal instrument dealing exclusively with women's rights was the *Convention on the Political Rights of Women*, adopted in 1952, which states that women shall be entitled to vote in all elections on equal terms with men, without any discrimination, and that women shall be entitled to hold public office and to exercise all public functions established by national law on equal terms with men.

Under the 1957 *Convention on the Nationality of Married Women*, each contracting State agrees that neither the celebration nor the dissolution of marriage between one of its nationals and an alien, nor the change of nationality of the husband during the marriage, shall automatically affect the nationality of the wife.

The 1962 *Convention on Consent to Marriage, Minimum Age for Marriage and Registration of Marriages*, and a 1965 Recommendation on the subject, aim especially at prohibiting child marriages and at safeguarding the principle of free consent to marriage.

The *Declaration on the Elimination of Discrimination against Women*, adopted by the Assembly in 1967, contains principles and standards relating to the rights of women in all spheres of family life and of society. These were included and expanded in the legally binding *Convention on the Elimination of All Forms of Discrimination against Women*, adopted by the Assembly in 1979. The Convention entered into force on 3 September 1981. Its purpose is to end the discrimination that denies or limits women's equality in political, economic, social, cultural and civic fields. States parties undertake to submit periodic reports on the measures they adopt to effect its provisions. The reports will be examined by the 23-member *Committee on the Elimination of Discrimination against Women*, elected by the States parties. The Committee held its first session in October 1982. It reports annually to the General Assembly.

See also The role of women in development *in* Chapter III.

Other human rights questions

Right to self-determination. The General Assembly has stressed the importance of the universal realization of the right of peoples to self-determination and of the speedy granting of independence to colonial countries and peoples for the effective guarantee and observance of human rights, and it has reaffirmed the legitimacy of the struggle of peoples for independence, territorial integrity, national unity and liberation from colonial and foreign domination and occupation by all available means, including armed struggle. In 1987, the Commission on Human Rights provided for the appointment of a special rapporteur to examine mercenarism as a way of violating human rights and impeding the exercise of the right to self-determination.

Economic, social and cultural rights. The Commission on Human Rights and its Sub-Commission on Prevention of Discrimination and Protection of Minorities have placed increasing emphasis on the realization of economic, social and cultural rights in connection with the guarantee of civil and political rights. Each year, the Commission reviews the situation regarding such rights, with a view to identifying obstacles of a general nature which impede their full realization and to suggesting steps that countries and the international community can take to overcome such obstacles. In 1986, the Commission considered reports from various specialized agencies on the state of implementation of the rights to food, health, education and work. It has also called for a study on the right to adequate food as a human right and has adopted resolutions on adequate housing.

Right to development. In 1986, the Assembly adopted the *Declaration on the Right to Development*, proclaiming that right to be an inalienable human right by virtue of each person and all peoples are entitled to participate in, contribute to and enjoy economic, social, cultural and political development in which all human rights and fundamental freedoms can be fully realized. The Declaration also states that the human person is the central subject of development and should be the active participant and beneficiary of the right to development.

Elimination of all forms of religious intolerance. The *Declaration on the Elimination of All Forms of Intolerance and of Discrimination Based on Religion and Belief*, adopted by the Assembly in 1981, states that everyone shall have the right of freedom of thought, conscience and religion and that no one shall be subject to discrimination on the grounds of religion or other beliefs.

In 1983, the Sub-Commission of the Commission on Human Rights appointed a special rapporteur to study the current dimensions of the problems of intolerance and discrimination on grounds of religion or belief, using the Declaration as the term of reference. The Commission, in 1986, appointed a special rapporteur to examine incidents and governmental actions inconsistent with the Declaration and to make recommendations in that regard.

Human rights and scientific and technological developments. The Assembly has called attention to human rights problems that may arise from developments in science and technology. A series of United Nations studies have examined the impact of science and technology on human rights, particularly the impact of advances in electronics, medicine and biology, as well as the negative consequences for human rights of environmental pollution and of the arms race.

The rights of the child. The Declaration of the Rights of the Child, adopted unanimously by the General Assembly in 1959, affirms the rights of the child to enjoy special protection and to be given opportunities and facilities to be able to develop in a healthy and normal manner. These and other rights of the child have been considered in the preparation, under way since 1978 in the Commission, of a draft convention on the rights of the child. *(See also section on* Assistance to children *in* Chapter III.)

Protection of women and children in armed conflicts. In 1974, the Assembly proclaimed the *Declaration on the Protection of Women and Children in Emergency and Armed Conflict*. The Declaration states that attacks and bombing on civilians, "especially on women and children, who are the most vulnerable members of the population", shall be prohibited and condemned and that States involved in armed conflicts shall make all efforts "to spare women and children from the ravages of war".

Protection of migrant workers. In 1979, the Assembly decided to establish a working group, open to all Member States, to elaborate an international convention on the protection of the rights of all migrant workers and their families.

Protection of indigenous populations. In 1982, the Sub-Commission established a Working Group on Indigenous Populations to review developments pertaining to, and give special attention to international standards concerning, the promotion and protection of the human rights of such populations. The Group is open and accessible to representatives of indigenous populations, organizations and Governments. In 1985, the Assembly established a *United Nations Voluntary Fund for Indigenous Persons*, to assist representatives of indigenous communities and organizations to take part in the Group's work.

The rights of aliens. In 1985, the Assembly adopted a *Declaration on the Human Rights of Individuals Who are not Nationals of the Country in which They Live*, recognizing certain rights enunciated in international instruments for citizens of a country that should also be ensured for non-nationals living there.

Other human rights questions of continuing concern to the United Nations include: protection of minorities; the question of conscientious objection to military service; human rights in the administration of justice, and the question of the abolition of the death penalty; the right and responsibility of individuals and groups to promote and protect human rights; and measures to be taken against totalitarian ideologies and practices based on racial intolerance, hatred and terror.

CHAPTER V

The United Nations at work for decolonization

More than 80 nations whose peoples were formerly under colonial rule have joined the United Nations as sovereign independent States since the world Organization was founded in 1945. In that historic change, the United Nations has played a crucial role by encouraging the aspirations of dependent peoples and by setting goals and standards to accelerate their attainment of independence.

The decolonization efforts of the United Nations derive from the Charter principle of "equal rights and self-determination of peoples", as well as from three specific chapters in the Charter—XI, XII and XIII—devoted to the interests of dependent peoples. Since 1960, the United Nations has also been guided by the General Assembly's Declaration on the Granting of Independence to Colonial Countries and Peoples (resolution 1514(XV)), by which Member States proclaimed the necessity of bringing colonialism to a speedy end.

Despite the great progress made against colonialism, over 3 million people still live under colonial rule, and the United Nations continues its efforts to help achieve self-determination and independence in the remaining dependent Territories.

International Trusteeship System

Under Chapter XII of the Charter, the United Nations established the International Trusteeship System for the supervision of Trust Territories placed under it by individual agreements with the States administering them. The System applied to: (i) Territories then held under Mandates established by the League of Nations after the First World War; (ii) Territories detached from enemy States as a result of the Second World War; and (iii) Territories voluntarily placed under the System by States responsible for their administration. The basic objective of the System was to promote the political, economic and social advancement of the Trust Territories and their progressive development towards self-government or independence.

The **Trusteeship Council** was established under Chapter XIII of the Charter to supervise the administration of Trust Territories and to ensure that Governments responsible for their administration took adequate steps to prepare them for the achievement of the Charter goals.

In the early years of the United Nations, 11 Territories were placed under the Trusteeship System: the 10 listed below and the Trust Territory of the Pacific Islands. The last Trust Territory (also known as Micronesia)—comprising the former Japanese-mandated islands of the Marshalls, the Marianas (with the exception of Guam) and the Carolines—is a strategic Trust Territory administered by the United States under an agreement approved by the Security Council in 1947.

By 1975, all except the Trust Territory of the Pacific Islands had either attained independence or were united with a neighbouring State to form an independent country, as follows:

Togoland under British administration	United with the Gold Coast (Colony and Protectorate), a Non-Self-Governing Territory administered by the United Kingdom, in 1957 to form Ghana
Somaliland under Italian administration	United with British Somaliland Protectorate in 1960 to form Somalia
Togoland under French administration	Became independent as Togo in 1960
Cameroons under French administration	Became independent as Cameroon in 1960
Cameroons under British administration	The northern part of the Trust Territory joined the Federation of Nigeria on 1 June 1961 and the southern part joined the Republic of Cameroon on 1 October 1961
Tanganyika under British administration	Became independent in 1961 (in 1964, Tanganyika and the former Protectorate of Zanzibar, which had become independent in 1963, united as a single State under the name of the United Republic of Tanzania)
Ruanda-Urundi under Belgian administration	Voted to divide into the two sovereign States of Rwanda and Burundi in 1962
Western Samoa under New Zealand administration	Became independent as Samoa in 1962

Nauru, administered by Australia on behalf of Australia, New Zealand and the United Kingdom	Became independent in 1968
New Guinea, administered by Australia	United with the Non-Self-Governing Territory of Papua, also administered by Australia, to become the independent State of Papua New Guinea in 1975

Non-Self-Governing Territories

The Charter of the United Nations also addresses the issue of other Non-Self-Governing Territories not brought into the Trusteeship System.

The Declaration regarding Non-Self-Governing Territories (Chapter XI of the Charter) provides that Members of the United Nations which administer Territories whose peoples have not attained a full measure of self-government recognize the principle that the interests of the inhabitants of those Territories are paramount and accept as a sacred trust the obligation to promote to the utmost the well-being of the inhabitants.

To this end, administering Powers, in addition to ensuring the political, economic, social and educational advancement of the peoples, as well as their just treatment, undertake to develop self-government, to take due account of the political aspirations of the peoples and to assist them in the progressive development of their free political institutions. Administering Powers are obliged to transmit regularly to the Secretary-General statistical and other information on the economic, social and educational conditions in their respective Territories.

In 1946, eight Member States—Australia, Belgium, Denmark, France, the Netherlands, New Zealand, the United Kingdom and the United States—enumerated the Territories under their administration which they considered to be non-self-governing and undertook to send information on them to the United Nations. In all, 72 Territories were enumerated, of which eight became independent in th period 1946-1959. Transmission of information was discontinued for 21 others for a variety of reasons, while several countries which attained independence in this period had never been included in the 1946 list.

Spain, which became a Member of the United Nations in 1955, began transmitting information in 1961 on the Territories under its

TERRITORIES TO WHICH THE DECLARATION ON DECOLONIZATION CONTINUES TO APPLY
(as at 30 June 1987)

Territory	Administering Authority
Africa:	
Namibia	United Nations[1]
Western Sahara	Spain[2]
Asia and the Pacific:	
American Samoa	United States
East Timor	Portugal[3]
Guam	United States
New Caledonia[4]	France
Pitcairn	United Kingdom
Tokelau	New Zealand
Trust Territory of the Pacific Islands	United States
Atlantic Ocean, Caribbean and Mediterranean:	
Anguilla	United Kingdom
Bermuda	United Kingdom
British Virgin Islands	United Kingdom
Cayman Islands	United Kingdom
Falkland Islands (Malvinas)	United Kingdom
Gibraltar	United Kingdom
Montserrat	United Kingdom
St. Helena	United Kingdom
Turks and Caicos Islands	United Kingdom
United States Virgin Islands	United States

---

[1] In 1966, the General Assembly terminated South Africa's mandate over South West Africa and placed the Territory under the direct responsibility of the United Nations. In 1968, the Assembly declared that the Territory would henceforth be known as Namibia, in accordance with the wishes of its people. Until independence, the legal Administering Authority for Namibia is the United Nations Council for Namibia.

[2] On 26 February 1976, Spain informed the Secretary-General that as of that date it had terminated its presence in the Territory of the Sahara and deemed it necessary to place the following on record: Spain considers itself henceforth exempt from any responsibility of an international nature in connection with the administration of the Territory, in view of the cessation of its participation in the temporary administration established for the Territory. On 5 December 1984, theGeneral Assembly reaffirmed that the question of Western Sahara was a question of decolonization which remained to be completed by the people of Western Sahara.

[3] On 20 April 1977, Portugal informed the Secretary-General that effective exercise of its sovereignty over the Territory had ceased in August 1975 and that the only information that could be transmitted would concern the first months of 1975. In subsequent years, Portugal further informed the Secretary-General that conditions prevailing in East Timor continued to prevent it from assuming its responsibilities for the administration of the Territory.

[4] On 2 December 1986, the General Assembly considered that New Caledonia was a Non-Self-Governing Territory within the meaning of Chapter XI of the Charter of the United Nations.

administration. In 1960, the Assembly determined that nine Territories administered by Portugal, which had become a Member of the United Nations in 1955, should be considered to be non-self-governing and requested Portugal to transmit information on those Territories. The list of Non-Self-Governing Territories was subsequently expanded to include Southern Rhodesia (now the independent State of Zimbabwe), South West Africa (Namibia), French Somaliland (later known as the French Territory of the Afars and the Issas), Comoro Archipelago and New Caledonia.

Declaration on the Granting of Independence to Colonial Countries and Peoples

The urgent demands of dependent peoples to be free of colonial domination and the international community's perception that Charter principles were being too slowly applied led to the General Assembly's proclamation in December 1960 of the Declaration on the Granting of Independence to Colonial Countries and Peoples (resolution 1514(XV)).

The Declaration states that the subjection of peoples to alien subjugation, domination and exploitation constitutes a denial of fundamental human rights, is contrary to the Charter, and is an impediment to the promotion of world peace and co-operation, and that "immediate steps shall be taken, in Trust and Non-Self-Governing Territories or all other Territories which have not yet attained independence, to transfer all powers to the peoples of those Territories, without any conditions or reservations, in accordance with their freely expressed will and desire, without any distinction as to race, creed or colour in order to enable them to enjoy complete independence and freedom".

In 1961, the Assembly established a 17-member Special Committee—enlarged to 24 members in 1962—to examine the application of the Declaration, and to make suggestions and recommendations on the progress and extent of its implementation. Commonly referred to as the Special Committee of 24 on decolonization, its full title is the *Special Committee on the Situation with regard to the Implementation of the Declaration on the Granting of Independence to Colonial Countries and Peoples.*

In 1970, 1975, 1980 and 1985, in connection with the tenth, fifteenth, twentieth and twenty-fifth anniversaries of the adoption of the Declaration, the Assembly adopted a series of action plans and programmes aimed at expediting and speedily implementing the Declaration. The Assembly on those occasions called on the Committee to continue its examination of the compliance by all States with the Declaration and with other resolutions on decolonization. It also reiterated its request to the Committee to send visiting missions to the Territories and to meet at places where it could obtain first-hand information on the situation in those Territories.

The Assembly declared that the continuation of colonialism in all its forms, including racism and *apartheid*, was incompatible with the Charter, the Declaration and principles of international law. It called on Member States, in particular colonial Powers, to take steps with a view to the complete, unconditional and speedy eradication of colonialism in all its forms and manifestations and strict observance of the relevant provisions of the Charter, the Universal Declaration of Human Rights, and all other relevant resolutions and decisions of the General Assembly and Security Council.

In the more than two decades since the Declaration on decolonization was adopted in 1960, some 60 former colonial Territories, inhabited by more than 80 million people, have attained independence and joined the United Nations as sovereign Members.

In its consideration of the remaining colonial Territories, the General Assembly has each year reaffirmed that the continuation of colonialism in all its forms and manifestations is incompatible with the Charter, the Universal Declaration of Human Rights and the Declaration on decolonization, and poses a serious threat to international peace and security.

The Assembly has called upon the administering Powers to take all necessary steps to enable the dependent peoples of the Territories to exercise fully and without delay their inalienable right to self-determination and independence. It has also called upon the administering Powers to withdraw immediately and unconditionally their military bases and installations from colonial Territories and to refrain from establishing new ones, and it has condemned the continuing activities of foreign economic and other interests which are impeding the implementation of the Declaration.

The Assembly has also reaffirmed its recognition of the legitimacy of the struggle of the peoples under colonial and alien domination to exercise their right to self-determination and independence by all the necessary means at their disposal.

With regard to the smaller Territories, the Assembly has repeatedly reaffirmed that questions of territorial size, geographical location, size of population and limited natural resources should in no way delay the implementation of the Declaration.

TERRITORIES* THAT HAVE ATTAINED INDEPENDENCE OR HAVE BECOME INTEGRATED OR ASSOCIATED WITH INDEPENDENT STATES SINCE THE ADOPTION IN 1960 OF THE DECLARATION ON DECOLONIZATION

State or other entity	Year of independence or change of status	Former administering Power (and former name)
Angola	1975	Portugal
Antigua and Barbuda	1981	United Kingdom
Bahamas	1973	United Kingdom
Barbados	1966	United Kingdom
Belize	1981	United Kingdom (British Honduras)
Botswana	1966	United Kingdom (Bechuanaland)
Brunei Darussalam	1984	United Kingdom (Brunei)
Cape Verde	1975	Portugal
Cocos (Keeling) Islands	1984 [a]	Australia
Comoros	1975	France
Cook Islands	1965 [b]	New Zealand
Democratic Yemen	1967	United Kingdom (Aden)
Djibouti	1977	France (Territory of the Afars and the Issas)
Dominica	1978	United Kingdom
Equatorial Guinea	1968	Spain (Fernando Poo and Río Muni)
Fiji	1970	United Kingdom
Gambia	1965	United Kingdom
Goa and dependencies	1961 [c]	Portugal
Grenada	1974	United Kingdom
Guinea-Bissau	1974	Portugal (Portuguese Guinea)
Guyana	1966	United Kingdom (British Guiana)
Ifni	1969 [d]	Spain
Jamaica	1962	United Kingdom
Kenya	1963	United Kingdom
Kiribati	1979	United Kingdom (Gilbert Islands)
Lesotho	1966	United Kingdom (Basutoland)
Malawi	1964	United Kingdom (Nyasaland)
Malta	1964	United Kingdom
Mauritius	1968	United Kingdom
Mozambique	1975	Portugal
Niue	1974 [b]	New Zealand
North Borneo	1963 [e]	United Kingdom
Oman	1971	United Kingdom
Saint Kitts and Nevis	1983	United Kingdom
Saint Lucia	1979	United Kingdom
Saint Vincent and the Grenadines	1979	United Kingdom
Sao Tome and Principe	1975	Portugal
Sarawak	1963 [e]	United Kingdom
Seychelles	1976	United Kingdom
Sierra Leone	1961	United Kingdom
Singapore	1965	United Kingdom
Solomon Islands	1978	United Kingdom

125

State or other entity	Year of independence or change of status	Former administering Power (and former name)
Suriname	1975	Netherlands (Dutch Guiana)
Swaziland	1968	United Kingdom
Trinidad and Tobago	1962	United Kingdom
Tuvalu	1978	United Kingdom (Ellice Islands)
Uganda	1962	United Kingdom
Vanuatu	1980	France and United Kingdom (New Hebrides)
West New Guinea (West Irian)	1963 [f]	Netherlands
Zambia	1964	United Kingdom (Northern Rhodesia)
Zimbabwe	1980	United Kingdom (Southern Rhodesia)

* Does not include Trust Territories, which are listed in the preceding table.

[a] Integrated with Australia.

[b] Became fully self-governing in free association with New Zealand.

[c] Nationally united with India.

[d] Returned to Morocco.

[e] North Borneo and Sarawak joined the Federation of Malaya in 1963 to form the Federation of Malaysia.

[f] United with Indonesia.

The Assembly has urged the specialized agencies and other organizations of the United Nations system to extend all necessary moral and material assistance to peoples of colonial Territories and to their national liberation movements. It has also invited all States to make, or continue to make, offers of study and training facilities for inhabitants of Non-Self-Governing Territories, including scholarships and travel funds.

In respect of certain territories, such as East Timor, the Falkland Islands (Malvinas) and Western Sahara, the Assembly has entrusted the Secretary-General with specific tasks in assisting in and facilitating the process of decolonization, in accordance with the United Nations Charter and the objectives of the Declaration.

Namibia

Namibia—formerly known as South West Africa—is the only one of the seven African Territories once held under the League of Nations Mandate System that was not placed under the Trusteeship System. The General Assembly recommended in 1946 that South Africa do so, but South Africa refused. Instead of complying with the Assembly's recommendation, in 1949 South Africa informed the United Nations that it would no longer transmit information on the Territory, on the grounds that the Mandate had lapsed with the demise of the League.

In 1950, the International Court of Justice, in an advisory opinion requested by the General Assembly, held that South Africa continued to have international obligations for the Territory to promote to the utmost the material and moral well-being and social progress of the inhabitants as a sacred trust of civilization and that the United Nations should exercise the supervisory functions of the League of Nations in the administration of the Territory. South Africa refused to accept the Court's opinion and continued to oppose any form of United Nations supervision over the Territory's affairs.

In October 1966, the Assembly declared that South Africa had failed to fulfil its obligations under the Mandate and to ensure the well-being of the Territory's people, and had, in fact, disavowed the Mandate. The Assembly decided that the Mandate was therefore terminated, that South Africa had no other right to administer the Territory and that thenceforth the Territory came under the direct responsibility of the United Nations.

In 1967, at a special session convened for the purpose of discussing the question of South West Africa, the Assembly established the United Nations Council for South West Africa (later renamed the **United Nations Council for Namibia** when, in 1968, the Assembly proclaimed that, in accordance with the wishes of its people, the Territory would thenceforth be known as Namibia) to administer the Territory until independence.

Later the same year, in the face of South Africa's refusal to accept the Assembly's decision and to co-operate with the Council for Namibia, the Assembly recommended that the Security Council take measures to enable the Council to carry out its mandate.

In its first resolution on the question, in 1969, the Security Council recognized the termination of the Mandate by the Assembly, described the continued presence of South Africa in Namibia as illegal and called on South Africa to withdraw its administration from the Territory immediately. The following year, the Security Council explicitly declared for the first time that "all acts taken by the Government of South Africa on behalf of or concerning Namibia after the termination of the Mandate are illegal and invalid".

This view was upheld in 1971 by the International Court of Justice, which stated, in an advisory opinion requested by the Security Council, that the continued presence of South Africa in Namibia being illegal, South Africa was under obligation to withdraw its administration from Namibia immediately and thus put an end to its occupation of the Territory. South Africa, however, continued to refuse to comply with United Nations resolutions on the question of Namibia, and continued its illegal administration of the Territory, including the imposition of *apartheid* laws, the bantustanization of the Territory and the exploitation of its resources.

In 1973, the Assembly decided that 26 August, marking the start of the Namibian liberation struggle in 1966, should be observed each year as *Namibia Day.*

To secure for the Namibians "adequate protection of the natural wealth and resources of the Territory which is rightfully theirs", the Council for Namibia enacted in September 1974 a *Decree for the Protection of the Natural Resources of Namibia*. Under the Decree, no person or entity may search for, take or distribute any natural resources found in Namibia without the Council's permission, and any person or entity contravening the Decree may be held liable for damages by the future government of an independent Namibia.

The Council also established, in the same year, the *Institute for Namibia* (located in Lusaka, Zambia, until South Africa's withdrawal from Namibia) to provide Namibians with education and training to strengthen their freedom struggle and equip them to administer a free Namibia.

In 1976, the Security Council for the first time demanded that South Africa accept elections for the Territory of Namibia as a whole under the supervision and control of the United Nations so that the people might freely determine their future. It condemned South Africa's illegal and arbitrary application of racially discriminatory and repressive laws and practices in the Territory, its military build-up in Namibia and its use of the Territory as a base for attacks on neighbouring countries.

In the same year, the General Assembly condemned South Africa for organizing so-called constitutional talks at Windhoek designed to perpetuate the colonial oppression and exploitation of Namibia. It decided that any independence talks must be between the representatives of South Africa and the South West Africa People's Organization (SWAPO), the national liberation movement of Namibia, which the Assembly recognized as the sole and authentic representative of the Namibian people. Those talks, the Assembly declared, should be held under the auspices of the United Nations for the sole purpose of discussing ways to transfer power to the people of Namibia.

The Assembly decided to observe annually the week of 27 October as the *Week of Solidarity with the People of Namibia and Their Liberation Movement, SWAPO.*

The Assembly also launched a comprehensive assistance programme in support of the nationhood of Namibia, covering both the struggle for independence and the initial years of independence, and involving assistance by the specialized agencies and other organizations within the United Nations system.

The Assembly declared, in 1977, that South Africa's decision to annex Walvis Bay—the main port and vital economic avenue of Namibia—was illegal, null and void and an act of colonial expansion. It condemned the annexation as an attempt to undermine the territorial integrity of Namibia.

At a special session on Namibia in May 1978, the Assembly adopted a Declaration on Namibia and Programme of Action in Support of Self-Determination and National Independence for Namibia. Expressing full support for the armed liberation struggle of the people under the leadership of SWAPO, it stated that any negotiated settlement must be arrived at with the agreement of SWAPO and within the framework of United Nations resolutions.

THE UNITED NATIONS PLAN FOR NAMIBIAN INDEPENDENCE In July 1978, the Security Council met to consider a proposal by the five Western members of the Council—Canada, France, the Federal Republic of Germany, the United Kingdom and the United States—for a settlement of the Namibian question. The proposal comprised a plan for free elections to a Constituent Assembly under the supervision and control of a United Nations representative assisted by a United Nations Transition Assistance Group, which would include both civilian and military components.

The Council took note of the Western proposal and requested the Secretary-General to appoint a Special Representative for Namibia.

In September 1978, after approving a report by the Secretary-General based on his Special Representative's findings, the Council, by resolution 435(1978), endorsed the United Nations plan for the independence of Namibia and decided to establish, under its authority, the United Nations Transition Assistance Group (UNTAG) to assist the Special Representative to carry out his mandate—namely, to ensure the early independence of Namibia through free and fair elections under United Nations supervision and control.

The Secretary-General's report stated that the implementation of the United Nations plan would be carried out in three stages:

(1) cessation of all hostile acts by all parties;

(2) repeal of discriminatory or restrictive laws and the release of political prisoners and voluntary return of exiles and refugees; and

(3) holding of elections after a seven-month pre-electoral period, to be followed by the entry into force of the newly adopted Constitution and the consequent achievement of the independence of Namibia.

Since 1978, the General Assembly has continually reaffirmed that Security Council resolution 435(1978) is the only basis for a peaceful settlement, and has called for its immediate and unconditional implementation "without qualification or modification". It has condemned South Africa for obstructing the implementation of that resolution and other United Nations resolutions and for "its manoeuvres, in contravention of those resolutions, designed to consolidate its colonial and neo-colonial interests at the expense of the legitimate aspirations of the Namibian people for genuine self-determination, freedom and national independence in a united Namibia".

In furtherance of the objective of bringing to an end South Africa's illegal occupation of Namibia, the General Assembly has called upon all States to sever all relations with South Africa, and it has urged the Security Council to impose comprehensive mandatory sanctions against South Africa.

In 1983, the Security Council mandated the Secretary-General to consult with the parties concerned in order to secure speedy implementation of resolution 435(1978). South Africa, however, maintained that Namibian independence was linked to the withdrawal of Cuban troops from Angola, a position which the Council rejected in October 1983 and again in June 1985.

Also in June 1985, the Security Council condemned South Africa for its installation that month of a so-called interim government in Namibia, and declared the action illegal, null and void. The General Assembly, referring to the "interim government" in December of that year, called on the international community not to recognize or cooperate with any régime imposed on the Namibian people by South Africa in violation of United Nations resolutions.

The International Conference for the Immediate Independence of Namibia (Vienna, July 1986) and a special session of the Assembly two months later sought to mobilize further action to end South Africa's illegal occupation of Namibia and to put into effect the United Nations plan for Namibia's peaceful transition to independence.

In March 1987, the Secretary-General reported that all outstanding issues relevant to the United Nations plan, including the choice of an electoral system, had been resolved; the linkage pre-condition thus was the only obstacle to the implementation of the plan. He expressed the view that South Africa should urgently reconsider its position on linkage, to enable the United Nations to proceed with the implementation of resolution 435(1978).

CHAPTER VI

The United Nations at work for international law

Article 1 of the United Nations Charter calls for the adjustment or settlement of international disputes by peaceful means in conformity with the principles of justice and international law. Among the methods of peaceful settlement, the Charter specifies, in Article 33, arbitration and judicial settlement. Under Article 13, one of the General Assembly's functions is "encouraging the progressive development of international law and its codification".

Judicial settlement of disputes

Since the inauguration of the **International Court of Justice** in 1946, States have submitted over 50 cases to it, and 18 advisory opinions have been requested by international organizations. Fifteen of the cases submitted by States were for various reasons withdrawn or removed from the list, and in 10 cases, the Court found that it lacked jurisdiction to decide upon the merits. In the remaining cases to date, covering a wide range of topics, final Judgments have been rendered in all but four.

Some cases have involved questions of territorial rights. Thus, in 1953, in a case between France and the United Kingdom, the Court found that certain Channel islets were under British sovereignty. In another case (1959), the Court upheld the claims of Belgium to an enclave situated near its frontier with the Netherlands. In a case decided in 1960, the Court found that India had not acted contrary to the obligations imposed on it by the existence of Portugal's right of passage between enclaves. In 1975, the Court found in respect of Western Sahara that there had been legal ties of allegiance between the Sultan of Morocco and some of the tribes living in Western Sahara, as well as legal ties between the Mauritanian entity and the Territory. In the Court's opinion, however, those legal ties were not of such a nature as might preclude application of the "principle of self-determination through the free and genuine expression of the will of the peoples of the Territory" of Western Sahara. In October 1983, Mali and the Upper Volta (now Burkina Faso) submitted to a chamber of the Court the question of the delimitation of a part of the land frontier between the two States; the chamber delivered its Judgment on 22 December 1986, adopting the line of the frontier. El Salvador and Honduras referred a similar matter to a Court chamber earlier in 1986, final Judgment on which has not been rendered.

Other cases before the Court have involved the law of the sea. In 1949, the Court found Albania responsible for damage caused to British warships by mines in its territorial waters. The Court upheld the right of warships to innocent passage through international straits in time of peace, although it also found the United Kingdom had violated Albanian sovereignty by attempting to sweep the area clear of mines, after the initial damage had been caused, without Albania's permission. In a fisheries dispute between the United Kingdom and Norway, the Court held in 1951 that the method employed by Norway in delimiting its territorial waters was not contrary to international law. In 1969, at the request of Denmark, the Netherlands and the Federal Republic of Germany, the Court indicated the principles and rules of international law applicable to the delimitation of the areas of the North Sea continental shelf appertaining to each of them. In 1974, the Court found that Iceland was not entitled unilaterally to exclude the fishing vessels of the United Kingdom and the Federal Republic of Germany from areas between fishery limits agreed in 1961 and the 50-mile limit proclaimed by Iceland in 1972. In 1982, at the request of Tunisia and the Libyan Arab Jamahiriya, and in 1985, in a case referred to it by means of a special agreement between the Libyan Arab Jamahiriya and Malta, the Court indicated the principles and rules of international law applicable to the delimitation of the areas of the Mediterranean continental shelf appertaining to each of them respectively.

In 1981, Canada and the United States submitted to a chamber of the Court a question as to the course of the maritime boundary dividing the continental shelf and fisheries zones of the two countries in the Gulf of Maine area. A final Judgment has not been rendered.

Some other cases have involved questions of treaty interpretation in such matters as rights of asylum in Latin America (Colombia v. Peru, 1950) and the rights of United States nationals in Morocco (France v. United States, 1951). In 1955, the Court found that the claim of a naturalized Liechtenstein citizen who had no real link with that country could not be espoused by Liechtenstein against Guatemala. In 1970, the Court held that Belgium had no legal capacity to protect the interests of Belgian shareholders in a Canadian company which had been the subject of certain measures in Spain. On 6 February 1987, the United States instituted proceedings against Italy in respect of a dispute arising out of the requisition of an Italian company stated to have been owned by United States corporations. The Court constituted a special chamber to deal with the case.

In cases concerning the discharge of duties of the mandatory Power for the Territory of South West Africa (Namibia), the Court found in 1966 that Ethiopia and Liberia had not established any legal rights or interests in the claim they had brought against South Africa. Four of the advisory opinions given by the Court have also concerned Namibia. Three of these were requested by the General Assembly. In the first, the Court expressed the opinion in 1950 that South Africa continued to have international obligations under the Mandate despite the dissolution of the League of Nations. In 1955, the Court stated over South African objections that the Assembly was correct in treating decisions concerning South West Africa as "important questions" requiring a two-thirds majority vote. The following year, the Court stated that the oral hearing of petitioners by the Committee on South West Africa were admissible as a necessary means to enable the United Nations to perform its supervisory duties effectively. The fourth opinion, requested by the Security Council, was given in 1971, when the Court stated that the continued presence of South Africa in Namibia was illegal and that South Africa was under obligation to withdraw its administration and put an end to its occupation of the Territory.

Among other opinions requested by the General Assembly, one was given in 1949 on a question put after the assassination of the United Nations mediator in Palestine: the Court found that the United Nations had the capacity to maintain a claim against a State for injuries to an agent of the Organization. Another concerned the refusal of certain States to contribute to the expenses of peace-keeping operations in the Middle East and the Congo. The Court held in 1962 that the expenses in question should be borne by all Member States in accordance with the Charter. Five advisory opinions have concerned aspects of judgments of the administrative tribunals of the United Nations or the International Labour Organisation.

In 1973, Australia and New Zealand each brought a case against France concerning the deposit of radioactive fall-out from nuclear tests conducted by France in the atmosphere above the Pacific atoll of Mururoa. The Court first indicated that, pending a final decision,

France should avoid such tests and later (1974) delivered Judgments finding, on the basis of statements made by French authorities, that France had undertaken to refrain from atmospheric nuclear testing after 1974, so that the claims of the applicant States no longer had any object and the Court was no longer called upon to give decisions in the cases.

In the case brought by the United States against Iran concerning the seizure of its embassy in Teheran and the detention of its diplomatic and consular staff, the Court first indicated provisionally (December 1979) that the embassy should be immediately given back and the detained staff released, and subsequently (May 1980) found on the merits that Iran had violated its obligations to the United States, must release the hostages, hand back the embassy and make reparation. However, before the Court had occasion to fix the amount of the reparation, the case was withdrawn following agreement reached between the two States.

On 9 April 1984, Nicaragua filed an application instituting proceedings against the United States on the grounds that the United States was using military force against Nicaragua and intervening in its internal affairs, in violation of its sovereignty. The United States denied the Court's jurisdiction.

On 10 May, the Court rejected a United States request that the case be removed from its list and called on the United States to refrain from action against Nicaraguan ports and, in particular, the laying of mines. In a Judgment delivered on 26 November 1984, the Court found that it had jurisdiction to entertain the case and that Nicaragua's application was admissible.

On 27 June 1986, the Court handed down its ruling, having determined that the United States actions towards Nicaragua were in breach of its obligations under international law and that it was under an obligation to desist from those actions and to make reparation to Nicaragua.

Development and codification of international law

The **International Law Commission** was established by the General Assembly in 1947 to promote the progressive development of international law and its codification. The Commission, which meets annually, is composed of 34 members who are elected by the Assembly for five-year terms and who serve in their individual capacity, not as representatives of their Governments.

Most of the Commission's work consists of the preparation of drafts on topics of international law, some chosen by the Commission and others referred to it by the Assembly or the Economic and Social Council. When the Commission completes draft articles on a particular topic, the Assembly usually convenes an international conference of plenipotentiaries to incorporate the articles into a convention which is then opened to States to become parties. Thus, for example:

◇ in 1958, a United Nations conference approved four conventions on the law of the sea: the *Convention on the High Seas*, the *Convention on the Territorial Sea and Contiguous Zone*, the *Convention on Fishing and Conservation of the Living Resources of the High Seas* and the *Convention on the Continental Shelf*;

◇ in 1961, a conference approved the *Convention on the Reduction of Statelessness*;

◇ two conferences, held in Vienna in 1961 and 1963, respectively approved the *Vienna Convention on Diplomatic Relations* and the *Vienna Convention on Consular Relations*;

◇ a conference which met in Vienna in 1968 and again in 1969 approved a *Convention on the Law of Treaties*;

◇ draft articles, prepared by the Commission, *Convention on Special Missions* and a *Convention on the Prevention and Punishment of Crimes against Internationally Protected Persons, including Diplomatic Agents*, were not referred to an international conference but were considered directly by the Assembly, which adopted the conventions on both subjects in 1969 and 1973, respectively;

◇ in 1975, an international conference adopted the *Vienna Convention on the Representation of States in Their Relations with Organizations of a Universal Character*;

◇ another conference convened by the Assembly, which met in Vienna in April 1977 and again in August 1978, completed and adopted the *Vienna Convention on Succession of States in Respect of Treaties*;

◇ in April 1983, a United Nations conference adopted, at Vienna, a *Convention on the Succession of States in Respect of State Property, Archives and Debts*;

◇ in accordance with a 1984 Assembly decision, a United Nations conference met at Vienna in March 1986 and adopted the *Vienna Convention on the Law of Treaties between States and International Organizations or between International Organizations*.

In 1978, when the Commission approved draft articles on most-favoured-nation clauses, the Assembly decided to transmit them to Governments for their comments.

The current work of the Commission includes the codification and progressive development of the law of State responsibility; the law of the non-navigational uses of international watercourses; the status of the diplomatic courier and the diplomatic bag not accompanied by diplomatic courier; jurisdictional immunities of States and their property; international liability for injurious consequences arising out of acts not prohibited by international law; relations between States and international organizations (second part of the topic); and the draft code of crimes against the peace and security of mankind.

International trade law

In response to the need for the United Nations to play a more active role in removing or reducing legal obstacles to the flow of international trade, the General Assembly established the **United Nations Commission on International Trade Law (UNCITRAL)** in 1966 to promote the progressive harmonization and unification of the law of international trade. The 36-nation Commission, whose members represent the various geographical regions and the principal economic and legal systems of the world, reports annually to the Assembly and also submits its report to the United Nations Conference on Trade and Development for comments.

The Commission's functions include co-ordination of the work of international organizations active in the field of international trade law, promotion of wider participation in existing international conventions, and the preparation of new conventions and other instruments relating to international trade law. The Commission also offers training and assistance in international trade law, taking into account the special needs of the developing countries.

The Commission's attention has been principally directed to the study and preparation of uniform rules in the following fields: international sale of goods, international payments including a legal guide on electronic fund transfers, international commercial arbitration, and international legislation on shipping.

The *Convention on the Limitation Period in the International Sale of Goods*, the first to be prepared by the Commission, was adopted in 1974 by a United Nations conference of plenipotentiaries convened by the General Assembly; a 1980 Protocol amended the Convention. A similar international conference adopted the *United Nations Convention on the Carriage of Goods by Sea* (known as the "Hamburg Rules") in 1978; the Commission had approved the draft text in 1967. A third international conference, held in 1980, adopted the *United Nations Convention on Contracts for the International Sale of Goods*, referred to as the "Vienna Sales Convention". The *UNCITRAL Arbitration Rules* (1976), the *UNCITRAL Conciliation Rules* (1980) and the *Model Law on International Commercial Arbitration* (1985) are additional uniform rules prepared by the Commission.

The Commission is drafting a convention on international bills of exchange and international promissory notes. A working group on the new international economic order, whose work is directed to issues involving developing countries, has completed its work on a legal guide for drawing up international construction contracts for large industrial projects. A second group is formulating uniform legal rules on the liability of transport terminal operators. Other projects currently in progress include work on international procurement and the preparation of model rules for electronic fund transfers.

Other legal questions

Among other questions on which conventions have been adopted by the General Assembly or are in preparation are those concerning the taking of hostages, international terrorism and the use of mercenaries.

The *International Convention against the Taking of Hostages*, adopted by the Assembly in 1979, had been drafted by a special committee set up by the Assembly in 1976. The Convention obliges contracting States to either prosecute or extradite any person committing an act of hostage-taking, and to take measures to prevent hostage-taking.

In 1972, the Assembly established an *ad hoc* committee on international terrorism, which has held three sessions (in 1973, 1977 and 1979), and submitted to the Assembly in 1979 recommendations on practical measures of co-operation for the elimination of the problem of international terrorism. In 1980, the Assembly established an *ad hoc* committee to draft an international convention against the recruitment, use, financing and training of mercenaries, which has held six sessions and worked out a consolidated negotiating basis of a convention.

Another Assembly committee, established in 1977 and originally mandated to work on a treaty on the non-use of force in international relations as well as the peaceful settlement of disputes "or such other recommendations as the Committee deems appropriate", was instructed by the Assembly in 1986 to complete a draft declaration on the enhancement of the effectiveness of the principle of non-use of force in international relations; it will be before the Assembly at its regular 1987 session.

Replacing an *Ad Hoc* Committee on the Charter of the United Nations, set up in 1974, the Assembly's ***Special Committee on the Charter of the United Nations and on the Strengthening of the Role of the Organization*** has met in annual sessions since 1976 to consider suggestions and proposals regarding the Charter and the role of the Organization. At its 1987 session, as at previous sessions, the Special Committee considered the question of the maintenance of international peace and security—more specifically: the question of the prevention and removal of threats to peace and of situations that might lead to international friction or give rise to a dispute; and a proposal on the role of Member States and of the United Nations in the maintenance of international peace and security. It also continued its consideration of a proposal on the resort to a commission of good offices, mediation or conciliation, and reviewed the question of the rationalization of United Nations procedures.

CHAPTER VII

Intergovernmental agencies related to the United Nations

The intergovernmental agencies related to the United Nations by special agreements are separate, autonomous organizations which work with the United Nations and each other through the co-ordinating machinery of the Economic and Social Council.

Sixteen of the agencies are known as "specialized agencies", a term used in the United Nations Charter. They report annually to the Economic and Social Council. They are the following:

- ✧ International Labour Organisation (ILO)
- ✧ Food and Agriculture Organization of the United Nations (FAO)
- ✧ United Nations Educational, Scientific and Cultural Organization (UNESCO)
- ✧ World Health Organization (WHO)
- ✧ World Bank/International Bank for Reconstruction and Development (IBRD)
- ✧ International Development Association (IDA)
- ✧ International Finance Corporation (IFC)
- ✧ International Monetary Fund (IMF)
- ✧ International Civil Aviation Organization (ICAO)
- ✧ Universal Postal Union (UPU)
- ✧ International Telecommunication Union (ITU)
- ✧ World Meteorological Organization (WMO)
- ✧ International Maritime Organization (IMO)
- ✧ World Intellectual Property Organization (WIPO)
- ✧ International Fund for Agricultural Development (IFAD)
- ✧ United Nations Industrial Development Organization (UNIDO)

The International Atomic Energy Agency (IAEA), established in 1957 "under the aegis of the United Nations", reports annually to the General Assembly and, as appropriate, to the Security Council and the Economic and Social Council.

The General Agreement on Tariffs and Trade (GATT) is a multilateral agreement which lays down rules for international trade.

International Atomic Energy Agency

The Statute of the International Atomic Energy Agency (IAEA) was approved on 26 October 1956 at an international conference held at United Nations Headquarters, and the Agency came into existence in Vienna on 29 July 1957. On 14 November 1957, the General Assembly approved an agreement concerning IAEA's relationship with the United Nations.

Aims and activities. In accordance with its Statute, IAEA's two main objectives are to seek to accelerate and enlarge the contribution of atomic energy to peace, health and prosperity throughout the world, and to ensure, so far as it is able, that assistance provided by it or at its request or under its supervision or control is not used in such a way as to further any military purpose.

IAEA fosters and guides the development of peaceful uses of atomic energy, establishes standards for nuclear safety and environmental protection, aids member countries through technical cooperation and fosters the exchange of scientific and technical information on nuclear energy.

One of IAEA's main functions is to apply safeguards to ensure that nuclear materials and equipment intended for peaceful use are not diverted to military purposes. The IAEA safeguards system is primarily based on nuclear material accountancy, verified on the spot by IAEA inspectors. Various types of safeguards agreements can be concluded with IAEA. Those in connection with the Non-Proliferation Treaty and the Treaty of Tlatelolco (*see section on* Disarmament *in* Chapter II) require non-nuclear-weapon States to submit their entire nuclear-fuel-cycle activities to IAEA safeguards. In 1986, IAEA was also asked to administer similar safeguards in connection with the South Pacific Nuclear-Free-Zone Treaty drafted by the South Pacific Forum.

To promote the development of the peaceful uses of nuclear energy, IAEA advises and assists Governments, at their request, on atomic energy programmes. The main objective of its technical assistance programme is to promote the transfer of skills and knowledge so that recipient countries can carry out their atomic energy programmes more efficiently and safely. It provides advisers, equipment and training to member States, the majority of which are developing countries.

IAEA formulates basic safety standards for radiation protection and issues regulations and codes of practice on specific types of operations, including the safe transport of radioactive materials. It also facilitates emergency assistance to member States in the event of a radiation accident. Two IAEA-prepared international conventions—the *Convention on Early Notification of a Nuclear Accident* and the *Convention on Assistance in the Case of a Nuclear Accident or Radiological Emergency*—came into force respectively on 27 October 1986 and 26 February 1987.

An expanded safety programme was adopted covering the areas of safety of nuclear installations, radiation protection, human health, radioactive waste management, nuclear power and the nuclear fuel cycle.

Information on virtually every aspect of nuclear science and technology is collected and disseminated by IAEA through its International Nuclear Information System in Vienna. With UNESCO, it operates the International Centre for Theoretical Physics in Trieste, Italy, and maintains three laboratories for studies in basic nuclear physics applications and practical uses. It works with FAO in research on atomic energy in food and agriculture and with WHO on radiation in medicine and biology.

Administration. IAEA's policies and programmes are directed by the General Conference, composed of all 113 IAEA member States, which meets annually, and by a 35-member Board of Governors.

Director General: Hans Blix.

Headquarters: Vienna International Centre, P.O. Box 100, A-1400 Vienna, Austria.

International Labour Organisation

The International Labour Organisation (ILO) was established in 1919, under the Treaty of Versailles, as an autonomous institution associated with the League of Nations. An agreement establishing the relationship between ILO and the United Nations was approved on 14 December 1946, and ILO became the first specialized agency associated with the United Nations.

Aims and activities. The ILO works to promote social justice for working people everywhere. It formulates international policies and programmes to help improve working and living conditions; creates international labour standards to serve as guidelines for national authorities in putting these policies into action; carries out an extensive programme of technical co-operation to help Governments in making these policies effective in practice; and engages in training, education and research to help advance these efforts.

ILO is unique among world organizations in that workers' and employers' representatives have an equal voice with those of Governments in formulating its policies. The International Labour Conference is composed of delegates from each member country—two from the government and one each representing workers and employers. One of its most important functions is the adoption of conventions and recommendations which set international labour standards in such areas as freedom of association, wages, hours and conditions of work, workmen's compensation, social insurance, vacation with pay, industrial safety, employment services, and labour inspection.

Conventions create binding obligations—for member States that ratify them—to put their provisions into effect, while recommendations provide guidance for national policy, legislation and practice. Since ILO was founded, more than 300 conventions and recommendations have been adopted. ILO monitors the application of conventions by ratifying States and has a special procedure for investigating complaints of infringements of trade union rights.

Through its programme of technical co-operation, ILO experts assist member countries in such fields as vocational training, management techniques, manpower planning, employment policies, occupational safety and health, social security systems, co-operatives and small-scale handicraft industries.

Opportunities for study and training are offered at ILO's International Institute for Labour Studies, at Geneva, and the International Centre for Advanced Technical and Vocational Training, at Turin, Italy.

Administration. Between the annual sessions of the International Labour Conference, in which all 150 members are represented, the work of ILO is guided by the Governing Body, comprising 28 government members and 14 worker and 14 employer members.

Director-General: Francis Blanchard.

Headquarters: 4, route des Morillons, CH-1211 Geneva 22, Switzerland.

Food and Agriculture Organization of the United Nations

The Food and Agriculture Organization of the United Nations (FAO) was founded at a conference in Quebec on 16 October 1945. Since 1979, that date has been observed annually as *World Food Day*.

Aims and activities. The aims of FAO are to raise levels of nutrition and standards of living; to improve the production, processing, marketing and distribution of all food and agricultural products from farms, forests and fisheries; to promote rural development and improve the living conditions of rural populations; and, by these means, to eliminate hunger.

In carrying out these aims, FAO promotes investment in agriculture, better soil and water management, improved yields of crops and livestock, and the transfer of technology to, and the development of agricultural research in, developing countries. It promotes the conservation of natural resources, particularly plant genetic resources, and the rational use of fertilizers and pesticides; combats animal diseases; promotes the development of marine and inland fisheries and of new and renewable sources of energy, in particular rural energy; and encourages the rational use of forest resources. Technical assistance is provided in all these fields and in others such as nutrition, agricultural engineering, agrarian reform, development communications, remote sensing for natural resources, and the prevention of food losses.

Special FAO programmes help countries prepare for, and provide relief in the event of, emergency food situations. Its Global Information and Early Warning System provides current information on the world food situation and identifies countries threatened by shortages, to guide potential donors. Its Food Security Assistance Scheme is designed to assist developing countries set up national food reserves.

Other programmes aim at improving seed production and distribution in developing countries and assisting countries in the supply and use of fertilizers. There is also a programme to control African animal trypanosomiasis, a disease severely limiting survival of livestock in Africa.

FAO acts as the lead agency for rural development in the United Nations system. It gives individuals and organizations the opportunity to participate in rural development through the Freedom from Hunger/Action for Development programme. With the United Nations,

FAO sponsors the *World Food Programme*, which uses food commodities, cash and services contributed by United Nations Member States to back programmes of social and economic development, as well as for relief in emergency situations.

Administration. The General Conference of FAO, composed of all 158 member nations, meets every other year to determine the policy and approve the budget and work programme of FAO. The Council, consisting of 49 member nations elected by the Conference, serves as the governing body of FAO between sessions of the Conference.

Director-General: Edouard Saouma.

Headquarters: Via delle Terme di Caracalla, 00100 Rome, Italy.

United Nations Educational, Scientific and Cultural Organization

The constitution of the United Nations Educational, Scientific and Cultural Organization (UNESCO) was prepared by a conference convened in London in 1945. UNESCO came into being on 4 November 1946.

Aims and activities. UNESCO's primary aim is to contribute to peace and security in the world by promoting collaboration among nations through education, science, culture and communication.

To realize these aims, UNESCO expands and guides education so as to enable the people of every country to take their own development in hand more effectively; helps in establishing the scientific and technological foundations through which every country can make better use of its resources; encourages national cultural values and the preservation of cultural heritage so as to derive the maximum advantage from modernization without the loss of cultural identity and diversity; develops communication for a free flow and a wider and better-balanced dissemination of information; and promotes the social sciences as instruments for the realization of human rights, justice and peace.

In education, its major activity, UNESCO combines literacy programmes with a drive to make primary education universal and eliminate illiteracy's root causes. It also helps train teachers, educational planners and administrators and encourages local building and equipping of schools.

In the natural sciences, UNESCO's programmes include Man and the Biosphere; the programme of the Intergovernmental Oceanographic Commission; and the International Hydrological and International Geological Correlation programmes. In addition, through education and training programmes, UNESCO helps to correct the imbalance in scientific and technological manpower, 90 per cent of which is now concentrated in the industrialized countries.

In the social sciences, UNESCO has produced studies on such subjects as tensions leading to war, racism, the socio-economic factors of development, and the relationship between man and his environment.

UNESCO's cultural activities are concentrated chiefly on the stimulation of artistic creativity, the study and development of cultures, and the conservation of the world's inheritance of books, works of art and monuments, as well as the preservation of cultural identities and oral traditions.

In communications, UNESCO surveys needs and assists developing countries, through its International Programme for the Development of Communication, to set up infrastructures in that field. Efforts are being made to broaden international co-operation to bring about a new information order, through studies of the role of the media in establishing a new economic order, co-operation with regional news agencies, and symposia whose aim is to increase the flow of third world news.

Administration. The General Conference of UNESCO, composed of representatives of the 158 member countries, meets biennially to decide the policy, programme and budget of the organization. The Executive Board, consisting of 50 members elected by the General Conference, meets at least two times a year and is responsible for supervising the programme adopted by the Conference.

Director-General: Amadou-Mahtar M'Bow.

Headquarters: 7, Place de Fontenoy, 75007 Paris, France.

World Health Organization

The World Health Organization (WHO) came into being on 7 April 1948, when 26 United Nations Member States had ratified its constitution. The date is observed annually as *World Health Day*.

Aims and activities. WHO's objective is the attainment by all peoples of the highest possible level of health. Since 1977, when the World Health Assembly set "Health for All by the Year 2000" as WHO's overriding priority, a global strategy has been worked out to reach this goal. The strategy, which requires the combined efforts of Governments and people for its implementation, is based on the primary health care approach, involving eight essential elements: education concerning prevailing health problems; proper food supply and nutrition; safe water and sanitation; maternal and child health, including family planning; immunization against major infectious diseases; prevention and control of local diseases; appropriate treatment of common diseases and injuries; and provision of essential drugs.

WHO helps countries reinforce their health systems by building up infrastructure, particularly health manpower and including services for the individual, family and community, health institutions, systems for referring complex problems to more specialized services, and the provision of essential drugs and other supplies and equipment.

WHO also promotes the research required to develop appropriate technologies relating to all aspects of health, including nutrition, maternal and child care, environmental safety, mental health, control of specific diseases, accident prevention, medical care and rehabilitation.

Provision of safe drinking water and adequate waste disposal for all are objectives of the *International Drinking Water Supply and Sanitation Decade* (1981-1990), in which WHO plays a major role.

WHO is leading a world-wide campaign to provide effective immunization for all children by 1990 to prevent the six major communicable diseases of childhood—diphtheria, measles, poliomyelitis, tetanus, tuberculosis and whooping cough. It is also active in international efforts to combat the diarrhoeal diseases, killers of infants and young children.

Global research programmes administered by WHO include a special programme, in collaboration with the United Nations Development Programme (UNDP) and the World Bank, of research and training in tropical diseases (malaria, leprosy, schistosomiasis, filariasis, trypanosomiasis and leishmaniasis). Working in co-operation with the World Bank, FAO, UNDP and several donor countries, WHO is engaged in a massive programme to combat onchocerciasis, or river blindness, in western Africa. WHO also directs and co-ordinates a special programme and global strategy to prevent and control AIDS (acquired immune deficiency syndrome), first identified in 1981, with public information and education about the modes of transmission as major priorities.

Administration. The governing body of WHO is the World Health Assembly, on which all 166 member States are represented.

It meets annually to review the organization's work and decide on policy, programme and budget. The Executive Board has 31 members, designated by as many countries; it acts as the executive arm of the Assembly.

Director-General: Dr. Halfdan T. Mahler.

Headquarters: 20, avenue Appia, 1211 Geneva 27, Switzerland.

World Bank

The World Bank is a group of three institutions: the International Bank for Reconstruction and Development (IBRD), which was established on 27 December 1945, when 28 countries had signed the Articles of Agreement that had been drawn up at a United Nations monetary and financial conference of 44 Governments, held in 1944 at Bretton Woods, New Hampshire (United States); the International Finance Corporation (IFC), established in 1956; and the International Development Association (IDA), established in 1960.

The common objective of all three institutions is to help raise standards of living in developing countries by channelling financial resources to those countries from developed countries.

INTERNATIONAL BANK FOR RECONSTRUCTION AND DEVELOPMENT

Aims and activities. The IBRD was established to assist in the reconstruction and development of territories of members by facilitating the investment of capital for productive purposes; to promote private foreign investment and, when private capital is not readily available on reasonable terms, to supplement private investment by providing finance for productive purposes; and to promote the long-range balanced growth of international trade and the maintenance of equilibrium in balances of payments by encouraging international investment for the development of productive resources of members.

The Bank's charter spells out the basic rules that govern its operations: it must lend only for productive purposes (such as agriculture and rural development, energy, education, health, family planning and nutrition, roads and railways, telecommunications, urban ports and power facilities) and must pay due regard to the prospects for repayment; each loan must be guaranteed by the Government concerned and, except in special circumstances, must be for specific

148

projects; the Bank must assure itself that the necessary funds are un-available from other sources on reasonable terms; the use of loans cannot be restricted to purchases in any particular member country or countries; and the Bank's decisions to lend must be based only on economic considerations. Since 1980, the Bank has made loans supporting programmes of specific policy changes and institutional reforms.

The Bank, whose capital is subscribed by its member countries, finances its lending operations primarily from its own borrowings in the world markets, as well as from retained earnings and the flow of repayments on its loans. Loans may be made to member coun-tries, to their political subdivisions or to private business enterprises in their territories. In addition to granting loans, the Bank provides a wide range of technical assistance services.

Administration. All powers of the Bank are vested in the Board of Governors, composed of one Governor and one alternate appointed by each of the 151 member countries. The Board normally meets once a year. There are 21 Executive Directors—five appointed by mem-bers having the largest number of shares and 16 elected by Gover-nors of the remaining members. The Board of Governors delegates to the Executive Directors authority to exercise all powers of the Bank, except those reserved to the Board by the Articles of Agreement. The President of the Bank is selected by the Board of Governors, of which he is *ex officio* Chairman.

INTERNATIONAL DEVELOPMENT ASSOCIATION

Aims and activities. The need for lending to many poor coun-tries on much easier terms than the Bank alone could give became apparent in the 1950s, and IDA was therefore established in 1960, as an affiliate of the Bank, to help meet this need.

The bulk of IDA's resources comes from three sources: transfers from the Bank's net earnings; capital subscribed in convertible cur-rencies by the 135 member countries of IDA; and contributions from IDA's richer members.

In order to borrow from IDA, a country must meet four criteria: it must be very poor (the "poverty ceiling" was $796 per capita gross national product in 1981 dollars); it must have sufficient economic, financial and political stability to warrant long-term development lend-ing; it must have an unusually difficult balance-of-payments problem and little prospect of earning enough foreign exchange to justify borrowing all it needs on conventional terms; and it must have a genuine commitment to development as reflected in its policies.

Nearly all IDA "credits", as they are called to distinguish them from Bank "loans", have been for a period of 50 years, without interest, except for a small charge to cover administrative costs. Repayment of principal does not begin until after a 10-year grace period.

Administration. The World Bank is responsible for the administration of IDA, and the Bank's Board of Governors, Executive Directors and President serve *ex officio* in IDA, which has 135 members.

INTERNATIONAL FINANCE CORPORATION

Aims and activities. While closely associated with the Bank, IFC is a separate legal entity and its funds are distinct from those of the Bank. Its aims are: to assist in financing private enterprise which could contribute to development by making investments, without guarantee of repayment by the member Government concerned; to bring together investment opportunities, domestic and foreign capital, and experienced management; and to stimulate the flow of private capital, domestic and foreign, into productive investment in member countries.

IFC's investments have been primarily in manufacturing but have included mining and energy, tourism, utilities and projects related to agriculture. Its resources come mainly from subscriptions by its 131 member countries and from accumulated earnings.

Administration. The Board of Governors, in which all powers of IFC are vested, consists of the Governors and alternates of the World Bank who represent countries which are also members of IFC. The Board of Directors, composed *ex officio* of the Executive Directors of the World Bank who represent countries which are also members of IFC, supervises the general operations of IFC. The President of the World Bank serves *ex officio* as Chairman of the Board of Directors of IFC.

President of the World Bank: Barber B. Conable, Jr.

Headquarters: 1818 H Street, N.W., Washington, D.C. 20433, United States.

International Monetary Fund

The Articles of Agreement of the International Monetary Fund (IMF) were drawn up, along with those of IBRD, at the 1944 Bretton Woods conference, and IMF came into being on 27 December 1945, when representatives of countries whose quotas amounted to 80 per cent of the Fund's resources had deposited their ratifications of the Agreement. The Articles have been twice amended, in 1969 and in 1978.

Aims and activities. The Fund seeks to promote international monetary co-operation and to facilitate the expansion of trade, and thus to contribute to increased employment and improved economic conditions in all member countries.

To achieve its purposes, IMF makes financing available to members in balance-of-payments difficulties and provides them with technical assistance to improve their economic management. Member countries undertake to collaborate with the Fund and with each other to assure orderly exchange arrangements and a stable system of exchange rates, together with a multilateral system of payments that is free from restrictions and thus promotes balance in the payments among countries.

The Fund maintains a pool of financial resources that it makes available to member countries to enable them to carry out economic reform programmes to remedy their payments deficits. Members make repayments to IMF so that its resources are used on a revolving basis and are continuously available to countries facing payments difficulties.

The Fund's special drawing rights (SDRs) are an international currency, created by IMF in 1969 under the first amendment to the Articles of Agreement. They can be used by its members for making international payments—for example, to obtain currency in a spot transaction, for the settlement of a financial obligation, as a loan or as security for a loan.

Administration. Each of the 151 member countries is represented by a Governor and an alternate Governor on the Board of Governors, the Fund's highest authority, which meets annually. A member country's voting power primarily reflects its contribution to the Fund's financial resources, which, in turn, is related to its relative size in the world economy. The daily business of IMF is conducted by an Executive Board of 21 Executive Directors, chaired by the Managing Director.

Managing Director: Michel Camdessus.

International Civil Aviation Organization

The International Civil Aviation Organization (ICAO) was established on 4 April 1947, after 26 States had ratified the Convention on International Civil Aviation which had been drawn up at the Chicago International Civil Aviation Conference in 1944.

Aims and activities. ICAO's objectives are to ensure the safe and orderly growth of international civil aviation throughout the world; encourage the arts of aircraft design and operation for peaceful purposes and the development of airways, airports and air navigation facilities for international civil aviation; and meet the needs of the peoples of the world for safe, regular, efficient and economical air transport.

ICAO has adopted, as annexes to the Chicago Convention, international standards and recommended practices for the safety, regularity and efficiency of air navigation and for the facilitation of air transport. These standards and recommended practices govern the performance of airline pilots, flight crews, air traffic controllers and ground maintenance crews, and also specify the design and performance of aircraft and much of its equipment. The rules of the air—both visual and instrument flight rules—by which pilots fly are formulated by ICAO, as are the aeronautical charts used for navigation throughout the world. Aircraft telecommunications systems—radio frequencies and security procedures—are also ICAO's responsibility.

ICAO works to facilitate international air transport through the reduction of procedural formalities—involving customs, immigration, public health—in the path of free and unimpeded passage of an aircraft, its passengers, crews, baggage, cargo and mail across international boundaries. It also meets requests for civil aviation assistance from developing countries in establishing or improving air transport systems and in training aviation personnel.

Administration. The ICAO Assembly, composed of delegates from all 156 member States, meets at least once every three years. It decides ICAO policy and examines any matters not specifically referred to the Council.

The Council, composed of representatives of 33 nations elected by the Assembly, is the executive body of ICAO. It carries out Assembly directives and administers the ICAO finances. It adopts standards for, and compiles, examines and publishes information on, international air navigation. It may act, if requested by the member States concerned, as a tribunal for the settlement of any dispute relating to international civil aviation.

President of the Council: Dr. Assad Kotaite.

Secretary-General: Yves Lambert.

Headquarters: 1000 Sherbrooke Street West, Suite 400, Montreal, Quebec H3A 2R2, Canada.

Universal Postal Union

The Universal Postal Union (UPU) was established on 9 October 1874 by the Berne Treaty, which was approved by 22 nations at Berne, Switzerland, and came into force on 1 July 1875. UPU became a specialized agency of the United Nations under the terms of an agreement which became effective on 1 July 1948.

Aims and activities. UPU forms a single postal territory of countries for the reciprocal exchange of letter-post items. Its objectives are to secure the organization and improvement of the postal services; to take part in postal technical assistance sought by the member countries of the Union; and to promote international collaboration in postal matters. Every member State of the UPU agrees to transmit the mail of all other members by the best means used for its own mail.

UPU fixes the rates, the maximum and minimum weight and size limits and the conditions of acceptance of letter-post items, which include letters (including aerogrammes), postcards, printed matter, literature in raised relief for the blind, and small packets. It also prescribes the methods for calculating and collecting transit charges (for letter-post items passing through the territories of one or more countries) and terminal dues (for imbalance of mails). In addition, it establishes regulations for registered and air mail and for objects of transport which require special precautions, such as infectious and radioactive substances.

UPU's technical co-operation projects include planning, organization, management, operations, training and financial services. The aid provided, primarily to meet the needs of developing countries, consists in recruiting and sending experts, UPU consultants or volunteers, granting vocational training or further training fellowships for individual or group courses, and supplying equipment and training or demonstration aids.

Administration. The Universal Postal Congress, composed of representatives of all member countries, is the supreme authority of UPU. It meets every five years to review the Universal Postal Convention and its subsidiary agreements on the basis of proposals submitted by member countries. The twentieth Congress is scheduled to take place in Washington in 1989.

The Executive Council, composed of 40 members elected by the Congress with due regard for equitable geographical distribution, meets annually to ensure the continuity of the work of the Union between congresses.

The Consultative Council for Postal Studies, composed of 35 members elected by the Congress, carries out studies and gives opinions on technical, operational and economic questions concerning the postal service, and also examines technical co-operation problems arising in the new and developing countries.

Director-General: A. C. Botto de Barros.

Headquarters: Weltpoststrasse 4, Berne, Switzerland.

International Telecommunication Union

The International Telecommunication Union (ITU) was founded at Paris in 1865 as the International Telegraph Union. Its name was changed to the International Telecommunication Union in 1934, following the adoption of the International Telecommunication Convention at Madrid in 1932. ITU became the United Nations specialized agency for telecommunications in 1947 as a result of an agreement concluded between the United Nations and the plenipotentiaries of the Union.

Aims and activities. The purposes of ITU are to maintain and extend international co-operation for the improvement and rational use of telecommunications of all kinds, to promote the development of technical facilities and their most efficient operation with a view to improving the efficiency of telecommunication services, increasing their usefulness and making them generally available to the public, and to harmonize the actions of nations in the attainment of these objectives.

To this end, ITU effects the allocation of the radio frequency spectrum and registration of radio frequency assignments in order to avoid

154

harmful interference between radio stations of different countries and to improve the use made of the radio frequency spectrum, It also effects an orderly recording of the positions assigned by countries to geostationary satellites. ITU co-ordinates efforts aimed at harmonizing the development of telecommunications facilities, notably those using space techniques, so as to take full advantage of their possibilities. It fosters collaboration among its members aimed at establishing rates at levels as low as possible consistent with an efficient service.

ITU also fosters the creation and improvement of telecommunication equipment and networks in developing countries through technical co-operation activities; promotes the adoption of measures for ensuring the safety of life through the co-operation of telecommunication services; undertakes studies, makes regulations and formulates recommendations and opinions; and collects and publishes information concerning telecommunications matters.

Administration. The supreme organ of ITU is the Plenipotentiary Conference, which meets normally every five years and is responsible for laying down ITU's basic policy. In addition, administrative conferences are convened to consider specific telecommunications matters, either world-wide or regional, and to adopt treaty-obligation-level agreements.

The Administrative Council, composed of 41 members of the Union elected by the Plenipotentiary Conference with due regard for equitable geographical representation, meets annually; it co-ordinates the work of the four permanent organs at ITU headquarters: the General Secretariat, the International Frequency Registration Board, the International Radio Consultative Committee and the International Telegraph and Telephone Consultative Committee.

Secretary-General: Richard E. Butler.

Headquarters: Place des Nations, 1211 Geneva 20, Switzerland.

World Meteorological Organization

The World Meteorological Organization (WMO) had its origin in the International Meteorological Organization, established in 1873. IMO was succeeded by the intergovernmental World Meteorological Organization. WMO's Convention was drawn up at a conference in Washington, D.C., in 1947 and came into force on 23 March 1950.

Aims and activities. WMO's aims are to aid in the establishment of networks of stations and centres to provide meteorological and hydrological observations and services; to promote the establishment and maintenance of systems for the rapid exchange of meteorological and related information; to promote standardization of meteorological and related observations and ensure the uniform publication of observations and statistics; to further the application of meteorology to aviation, shipping, water problems, agriculture and other activities; to promote activities in operational hydrology and to further co-operation between meteorological and hydrological services; and to encourage research and training in meteorology and related fields.

WMO has implemented the establishment of the "World Weather Watch", using surface-based observations, meteorological satellites and a system of world and regional meteorological centres operated by national weather services of members. In recent years, with atmospheric and oceanic data obtained from space fast becoming the basis of extended-range weather forecasts for the entire globe, WMO has given high priority to space-based observational systems.

WMO's World Climate Programme, the outcome of the World Climate Conference (Geneva, 1979), seeks to improve knowledge of the natural variability of climate and the effects of climatic changes due either to natural causes or to human activities. Other WMO programmes include those on research and development, hydrology and water resources, education and training, technical co-operation and regional programmes.

Administration. The supreme body of WMO is the World Meteorological Congress, in which all members are represented normally by the heads of their meteorological services. It meets every four years to determine general policies for WMO. The Executive Council, composed of 36 directors of national meteorological or hydrological services serving in an individual capacity, meets at least once a year to supervise the programmes approved by the Congress.

There are six regional meteorological associations—for Africa, Asia, South America, North and Central America, Europe and the south-west Pacific—each composed of members whose task is to co-ordinate meteorological and related activites within their respective regions. Eight technical commissions, composed of experts designated by WMO members, are responsible for studying aeronautical, agricultural and marine meteorology, atmospheric sciences, basic systems, hydrology, instruments and methods of observation, and climatology.

Secretary-General: G.O.P. Obasi.

Headquarters: 41, avenue Giuseppe-Motta, 1211 Geneva 20, Switzerland.

International Maritime Organization

The convention establishing the International Maritime Organization (IMO) (formerly called the Inter-Governmental Maritime Consultative Organization) was drawn up in 1948 at a United Nations maritime conference held at Geneva. The convention came into force on 17 March 1958, when it was ratified by 21 States, including seven with at least 1 million gross tons of shipping each.

Aims and activities. The aims and purposes of IMO are to provide machinery for co-operation and exchange of information among Governments on technical matters affecting shipping engaged in international trade; to encourage the general adoption of the highest practicable standards in matters concerning maritime safety, efficiency of navigation and the prevention and control of marine pollution from ships; and to deal with legal questions related to those matters.

IMO provides a forum for member Governments and interested organizations to exchange information on, and discuss and endeavour to solve problems connected with, technical, legal and other questions concerning shipping and the prevention of marine pollution by ships. As a result of such discussions, IMO has adopted a number of conventions and recommendations which Governments have adopted and which have entered into force. Among these are international conventions for the safety of life at sea, the prevention of marine pollution by ships, the training and certification of seafarers and the prevention of collisions at sea.

In addition to formal treaty instruments, IMO has adopted several hundred recommendations dealing with a wide range of subjects, such as maritime dangerous goods, signals, safety for fishermen and fishing vessels and safety of nuclear merchant ships. While not legally binding, these recommendations constitute codes or recommended practices and provide guidance to Governments in framing national regulations.

Administration. The Assembly, consisting of all member States, is the supreme governing organ of IMO. It meets every two years to approve the biennial work programme and budget of IMO and to adopt recommendations on regulations concerning maritime safety, prevention of marine pollution and other matters.

The 32-member Council, elected by the Assembly for two-year terms, is the governing body between the biennial sessions of the Assembly.

There are four principal committees—on maritime safety, legal matters, marine environment protection and technical co-operation—which submit reports or recommendations to the Assembly through the Council.

Secretary-General: Chandrika Prasad Srivastava.

Headquarters: 4 Albert Embankment, London SE1 7SR, England.

World Intellectual Property Organization

The World Intellectual Property Organization (WIPO) had its origins in the 1883 Paris Convention for the Protection of Industrial Property and the 1886 Berne Convention for the Protection of Literary and Artistic Works. The Convention establishing WIPO was signed in 1967 and entered into force in 1970. WIPO became a specialized agency of the United Nations on 17 December 1974.

Aims and activities. The main objectives of WIPO are: to maintain and increase respect for intellectual property throughout the world, in order to favour industrial and cultural development by stimulating creative activity and facilitating the transfer of technology and the dissemination of literary and artistic works. Intellectual property comprises two main branches: industrial property, chiefly inventions, trade marks and industrial designs; and copyright, chiefly for literary, musical, artistic, photographic and cinematographic works.

To aid in the protection of intellectual property, WIPO promotes the wider acceptance of existing treaties and their revision and, where necessary, encourages the conclusion of new treaties and assists in the development of national legislation; gives legal technical assistance to developing countries; assembles and disseminates information; and maintains services for international registration or other administrative co-operation among the member States of the "Unions" which WIPO administers and which are founded on treaties, conventions and agreements dating back to 1883.

Administration. WIPO has a Conference of all member States and a General Assembly, composed of those member States which are also members of the Paris or Berne Unions. The governing bodies of WIPO and the Unions administered by WIPO normally meet in joint session to adopt their programmes and budgets and to discuss and decide policy.

Director General: Arpad Bogsch.

158

International Fund for Agricultural Development

The agreement establishing the International Fund for Agricultural Development (IFAD) was adopted on 13 June 1976 at a United Nations conference. It was opened for signature on 20 December 1976, following the attainment of initial pledges of $1 billion, and entered into force on 30 November 1977. The idea for IFAD was one of the major outcomes of the 1974 World Food Conference.

Aims and activities. The main purpose of IFAD is to mobilize resources to help developing countries improve their food production and nutrition. IFAD deals exclusively with agriculture—including livestock, fisheries, processing and storage—and concentrates on rural areas, where the vast majority of the people in the developing world live and work. Its primary goal is to help efforts to end the chronic hunger and malnutrition suffered by at least 20 per cent of the people of Africa, Asia and Latin America.

IFAD lends money—most of it on highly concessional or low-interest terms—for projects which will have a significant impact on improving food production in developing countries, particularly for the benefit of the poorest sections of the rural populations. It seeks to apply its resources as part of an effort to bring small farmers and the landless into the development process. Thus, IFAD is concerned not only with production objectives but with the impact each project may have on employment, nutrition and income distribution.

Loan operations of IFAD fall into two groups: projects initiated by IFAD and projects "co-financed" with other financial and development institutions, such as the World Bank and IDA and the various development banks (African, Asian, Inter-American, Islamic). IFAD loans represent only a part of total project costs; the Governments concerned contribute a share.

IFAD projects deal with agricultural and rural development, livestock development, irrigation, settlement, research/extension/training, credit and fisheries.

Administration. The Fund's operations are directed by the Governing Council, on which all member States are represented, each of the three categories of members (developed countries, oil-exporting developing countries and other developing countries) having the same number of votes. Thus, the donor countries hold two thirds of the total number of votes and the developing countries, at the same time, hold two thirds of the votes. Current operations are overseen by the Executive Board, composed of 18 Executive Directors, six from each of the three constituent categories, and 18 alternates, and chaired by the President of the Fund.

President: Idriss Jazairy.

Headquarters: Via del Serafico 107, 00142 Rome, Italy.

United Nations Industrial Development Organization

The United Nations Industrial Development Organization (UNIDO) was established by the United Nations General Assembly in 1966 as an organ to promote and accelerate the industrialization of the developing countries and to co-ordinate United Nations activities in this field. Its conversion to the status of a specialized agency, proposed by the Second General Conference of UNIDO (Lima, 1975), was given effect in 1979 when a conference of plenipotentiaries, meeting in Vienna, adopted a constitution for UNIDO. The document received the required number of ratifications on 21 June 1985; the Assembly approved an agreement between the United Nations and UNIDO on 17 December 1985; and, transitional arrangements having ended that month, UNIDO became a fully autonomous specialized agency on 1 January 1986.

Aims and activities. The organization is the United Nations system's central co-ordinating body in industrial development. Encouraging and assisting developing countries to promote and accelerate their industrialization, it co-ordinates, initiates, and follows up United Nations activities to this end. It also contributes to co-operation between industrialized and developing countries in accelerating world industrial development, providing a forum for contacts, consultations and negotiations between them, encourages investment promotion activities in this regard, and promotes and facilitates the transfer of technology to and among developing countries. UNIDO's system of consultations is a series of meetings where industrialized and developing countries come together to discuss ways to accelerate industrialization by encouraging the involvement of Governments and industry. On the basis of studies and surveys, UNIDO creates and develops concepts and approaches for industrial development and helps formulate plans in the public, co-operative and private sectors, including the advancement of enterprise-to-enterprise co-operation in these sectors, and assists in regional industrial development planning.

The organization provides technical assistance in industrial development, organizes industrial training programmes, provides advisory services and assists countries in obtaining fair and equitable external financing. As a clearing-house for industrial information, UNIDO collects, analyses, publishes, standardizes and improves industrial statistics.

Administration. The principal organs of UNIDO are: the General Conference, which determines the guiding principles, approves the budget and adopts conventions and agreements; the 53-member Industrial Development Board, which reviews Conference-approved programmes and makes recommendations; and the 27-member Programme and Budget Committee.

Director-General: Domingo L. Siazon, Jr.

Headquarters: Wagramerstrasse 5, Vienna XXII, Austria.

General Agreement on Tariffs and Trade

The General Agreement on Tariffs and Trade (GATT), in force since 1 January 1948, is the only multilateral instrument which lays down agreed rules for international trade. It is subscribed to by 94 countries (Contracting Parties), which together account for four fifths of world trade. Another country has acceded provisionally, and a further 30 apply the Agreement on a *de facto* basis.

Aims and activities. The basic aim of GATT is to liberalize world trade and place it on a secure basis, thereby contributing to economic growth and development and the welfare of the world's peoples.

It is the principal international body concerned with the reduction of trade barriers and other measures which distort competition, with the conciliation of trade disputes, and with international trade relations. It is also a major repository of trade information. GATT is in effect both a code of rules and a forum in which countries can discuss and overcome their trade problems and negotiate to enlarge world trading opportunities.

GATT's basic principles are: that trade should be conducted on the basis of non-discrimination (the "most-favoured-nation" clause); that where protection is given to domestic industry, it should be extended essentially through the customs tariff and not through other commercial measures; that tariffs should be reduced through multilateral negotiations and be "bound" against subsequent increase; and that Contracting Parties should consult together to overcome trade problems.

A special chapter of the General Agreement deals with trade and development, and other articles also recognize the special trade problems of developing countries. The *International Trade Centre*, established by GATT in 1964, assists developing countries in export promotion. Operated jointly with UNCTAD since 1968, it provides information and advice on export markets and marketing techniques and helps in establishing export services and training personnel.

Seven major negotiating conferences (known as "Rounds") in GATT have brought about far-reaching reductions in tariffs and other trade barriers. The most significant were the first (Geneva, 1947), the Kennedy (1964-67) and the Tokyo (1973-79) Rounds. The Tokyo Round brought about substantial tariff reductions affecting some $300 billion of world trade. Agreements were reached on subsidies and countervailing measures, technical barriers, import licensing procedures, customs valuation, revision of the GATT Anti-Dumping Code and agreements in trade of bovine meat and dairy products and in civil aircraft; new framework agreements created new understandings for developing countries; and trade barriers facing tropical products were reduced.

In September 1986, the GATT trade ministers at Punta del Este, Uruguay, launched the eighth Round. Negotiations, which started in 1987, aimed at a further liberalization of world trade in goods. The ministers also undertook to seek improvements to the GATT framework and to examine negotiation on trade in services.

Administration. The most senior body of GATT is the annual session of Contracting Parties. GATT decisions are generally arrived at by consensus, not by vote. Between sessions, the Council of Representatives is authorized to take action on both routine and urgent matters. Other GATT bodies are Committees on Trade and Development, on Balance-of-Payments Restrictions, and on Textiles, as well as the high-level Consultative Group of Eighteen. Major standing committees or councils supervise various Tokyo Round agreements or arrangements, and a committee deals with budgetary, financial and administrative questions. The highest body in the Uruguay Round is the Trade Negotiations Committee, under which are Groups of Negotiations on Goods and on Services, and a Surveillance Body which oversees implementation of commitments by the trade ministers to a "standstill" on trade measures inconsistent with GATT, and to a "rollback" programme for phasing out such measures.

Director-General: Arthur Dunkel.

Headquarters. Centre William Rappard, 154 rue de Lausanne, 1211 Geneva 21, Switzerland.

APPENDICES

LIST OF ABBREVIATIONS

ECA	Economic Commission for Africa
ECE	Economic Commission for Europe
ECLA	Economic Commission for Latin America and the Caribbean
ESCWA	Economic and Social Commission for Western Asia
ESCAP	Economic and Social Commission for Asia and the Pacific
FAO	Food and Agriculture Organization of the United Nations
GATT	General Agreement on Tariffs and Trade
IAEA	International Atomic Energy Agency
IBRD	International Bank for Reconstruction and Development (World Bank)
ICAO	International Civil Aviation Organization
IDA	International Development Association
IFAD	International Fund for Agricultural Development
IFC	International Finance Corporation
ILO	International Labour Organisation
IMF	International Monetary Fund
IMO	International Maritime Organization
INSTRAW	International Research and Training Institute for the Advancement of Women
ITU	International Telecommunication Union
UNCHS	United Nations Centre for Human Settlements (Habitat)
UNCTAD	United Nations Conference on Trade and Development
UNDOF	United Nations Disengagement Observer Force
UNDP	United Nations Development Programme
UNDRO	Office of the United Nations Disaster Relief Co-ordinator
UNEP	United Nations Environment Programme
UNESCO	United Nations Educational, Scientific and Cultural Organization
UNFICYP	United Nations Peace-keeping Force in Cyprus
UNFPA	United Nations Fund for Population Activities
UNHCR	Office of the United Nations High Commissioner for Refugees
UNICEF	United Nations Children's Fund
UNIDIR	United Nations Institute for Disarmament Research
UNIDO	United Nations Industrial Development Organization
UNIFIL	United Nations Interim Force in Lebanon
UNITAR	United Nations Institute for Training and Research
UNMOGIP	United Nations Military Observer Group in India and Pakistan
UNRISD	United Nations Research Institute for Social Development
UNRWA	United Nations Relief and Works Agency for Palestine Refugees in the Near East
UNSO	United Nations Sudano-Sahelian Office
UNTSO	United Nations Truce Supervision Organization
UNU	United Nations University
UNV	United Nations Volunteers
UPU	Universal Postal Union
WFC	World Food Council
WFP	World Food Programme
WHO	World Health Organization
WIPO	World Intellectual Property Organization
WMO	World Meteorological Organization

GROWTH OF UNITED NATIONS MEMBERSHIP, 1945-1987

Year	Number	Original Member States
1945	51	Argentina, Australia, Belgium, Bolivia, Brazil, Byelorussian Soviet Socialist Republic, Canada, Chile, China, Colombia, Costa Rica, Cuba, Czechoslovakia, Denmark, Dominican Republic, Ecuador, Egypt, El Salvador, Ethiopia, France, Greece, Guatemala, Haiti, Honduras, India, Iran, Iraq, Lebanon, Liberia, Luxembourg, Mexico, Netherlands, New Zealand, Nicaragua, Norway, Panama, Paraguay, Peru, Philippines, Poland, Saudi Arabia, South Africa, Syrian Arab Republic, Turkey, Ukrainian Soviet Socialist Republic, Union of Soviet Socialist Republics, United Kingdom of Great Britain and Northern Ireland, United States of America, Uruguay, Venezuela, Yugoslavia

Year	Number	New Member States
1946	55	Afghanistan, Iceland, Sweden, Thailand
1947	57	Pakistan, Yemen
1948	58	Burma
1949	59	Israel
1950	60	Indonesia
1955	76	Albania, Austria, Bulgaria, Democratic Kampuchea, Finland, Hungary, Ireland, Italy, Jordan, Lao People's Democratic Republic, Libyan Arab Jamahiriya, Nepal, Portugal, Romania, Spain, Sri Lanka
1956	80	Japan, Morocco, Sudan, Tunisia
1957	82	Ghana, Malaysia
1958	83	Guinea
1960	100	Benin, Burkina Faso, Cameroon, Central African Republic, Chad, Congo, Côte d'Ivoire, Cyprus, Gabon, Madagascar, Mali, Niger, Nigeria, Senegal, Somalia, Togo, Zaire
1961	104	Mauritania, Mongolia, Sierra Leone, United Republic of Tanzania
1962	110	Algeria, Burundi, Jamaica, Rwanda, Trinidad and Tobago, Uganda
1963	112	Kenya, Kuwait
1964	115	Malawi, Malta, Zambia
1965	118	Gambia, Maldives, Singapore
1966	122	Barbados, Botswana, Guyana, Lesotho
1967	123	Democratic Yemen
1968	126	Equatorial Guinea, Mauritius, Swaziland
1970	127	Fiji
1971	132	Bahrain, Bhutan, Oman, Qatar, United Arab Emirates
1973	135	Bahamas, Federal Republic of Germany, German Democratic Republic
1974	138	Bangladesh, Grenada, Guinea-Bissau
1975	144	Cape Verde, Comoros, Mozambique, Papua New Guinea, Sao Tome and Principe, Suriname
1976	147	Angola, Samoa, Seychelles
1977	149	Djibouti, Viet Nam
1978	151	Dominica, Solomon Islands
1979	152	Saint Lucia
1980	154	Saint Vincent and the Grenadines, Zimbabwe
1981	157	Antigua and Barbuda, Belize, Vanuatu
1983	158	Saint Kitts and Nevis
1984	159	Brunei Darussalam

UNITED NATIONS MEMBER STATES

(at 30 June 1987)

Member State	Date of Admission	Scale of Assessments (per cent)	Population (est.)
Afghanistan	19 November 1946	0.01	18,136,000
Albania	14 December 1955	0.01	2,962,000
Algeria	8 October 1962	0.14	21,718,000
Angola	1 December 1976	0.01	8,754,000
Antigua and Barbuda	11 November 1981	0.01	80,000
Argentina	24 October 1945	0.62	30,564,000
Australia	1 November 1945	1.66	15,752,000
Austria	14 December 1955	0.74	7,558,000
Bahamas	18 September 1973	0.01	235,000
Bahrain	21 September 1971	0.02	417,000
Bangladesh	17 September 1974	0.02	98,657,000
Barbados	9 December 1966	0.01	253,000
Belgium	27 December 1945	1.18	9,903,000
Belize	25 September 1981	0.01	166,000
Benin[a]	20 September 1960	0.01	3,932,000
Bhutan	21 September 1971	0.01	1,417,000
Bolivia	14 November 1945	0.01	6,547,000
Botswana	17 October 1966	0.01	1,128,000
Brazil	24 October 1945	1.40	135,564,000
Brunei Darussalam	21 September 1984	0.04	224,000
Bulgaria	14 December 1955	0.16	8,948,000
Burkina Faso[b]	20 September 1960	0.01	7,747,000
Burma	19 April 1948	0.01	37,153,000
Burundi	18 September 1962	0.01	4,718,000
Byelorussian Soviet Socialist Republic	24 October 1945	0.34	9,910,000
Cameroon	20 September 1960	0.01	10,446,000
Canada	9 November 1945	3.06	25,379,000
Cape Verde	16 September 1975	0.01	334,000
Central African Republic	20 September 1960	0.01	2,608,000
Chad	20 September 1960	0.01	5,018,000
Chile	24 October 1945	0.07	12,353,000
China[c]	24 October 1945	0.79	1,059,521,000
Colombia	5 November 1945	0.13	28,624,000
Comoros	12 November 1975	0.01	444,000
Congo	20 September 1960	0.01	1,740,000
Costa Rica	2 November 1945	0.02	2,489,000
Côte d'Ivoire	20 September 1960	0.02	9,810
Cuba	24 October 1945	0.09	10,219,000
Cyprus	20 September 1960	0.02	670,000
Czechoslovakia	24 October 1945	0.70	15,480,000
Democratic Kampuchea[d]	14 December 1955	0.01	7,284,000
Democratic Yemen	14 December 1967	0.01	2,294,000
Denmark	24 October 1945	0.72	5,116,000
Djibouti	20 September 1977	0.01	430,000
Dominica	18 December 1978	0.01	76,000
Dominican Republic	24 October 1945	0.03	6,243,000
Ecuador	21 December 1945	0.03	9,378,000

Member State	Date of Admission	Scale of Assessments (per cent)	Population (est.)
Egypt[e]	24 October 1945	0.07	48,761,000
El Salvador	24 October 1945	0.01	4,819,000
Equatorial Guinea	12 November 1968	0.01	392,000
Ethiopia	13 November 1945	0.01	43,350,000
Fiji	13 October 1970	0.01	702,000
Finland	14 December 1955	0.50	4,915,000
France	24 October 1945	6.37	55,172,000
Gabon	20 September 1960	0.03	1,206,000
Gambia	21 September 1965	0.01	643,000
German Democratic Republic	18 September 1973	1.33	16,644,000
Germany, Federal Republic of	18 September 1973	8.26	61,017,000
Ghana	8 March 1957	0.01	13,588,000
Greece	25 October 1945	0.44	9,935,000
Grenada	17 September 1974	0.01	112,000
Guatemala	21 November 1945	0.02	7,963,000
Guinea	12 December 1958	0.01	6,075,000
Guinea-Bissau	17 September 1974	0.01	890,000
Guyana	20 September 1966	0.01	790,000
Haiti	24 October 1945	0.01	5,358,000
Honduras	17 December 1945	0.01	4,372,000
Hungary	14 December 1955	0.22	10,628,000
Iceland	19 November 1946	0.03	241,000
India	30 October 1945	0.35	750,900,000
Indonesia	28 September 1950	0.14	165,155,000
Iran (Islamic Republic of)	24 October 1945	0.63	44,919,000
Iraq	21 December 1945	0.12	15,898,000
Ireland	14 December 1955	0.18	3,552,000
Israel	11 May 1949	0.22	4,281,000
Italy	14 December 1955	3.79	57,186,000
Jamaica	18 September 1962	0.02	2,337,000
Japan	18 December 1956	10.84	121,470,000
Jordan	14 December 1955	0.01	3,515,000
Kenya	16 December 1963	0.01	20,333,000
Kuwait	14 May 1963	0.29	1,791,000
Lao People's Democratic Republic	14 December 1955	0.01	4,117,000
Lebanon	24 October 1945	0.01	2,668,000
Lesotho	17 October 1966	0.01	1,528,000
Liberia	2 November 1945	0.01	2,189,000
Libyan Arab Jamahiriya	14 December 1955	0.26	3,605,000
Luxembourg	24 October 1945	0.05	366,000
Madagascar	20 September 1960	0.01	9,985,000
Malawi	1 December 1964	0.01	7,059,000
Malaysia[f]	17 September 1957	0.10	15,557,000
Maldives	21 September 1965	0.01	177,000
Mali	28 September 1960	0.01	8,206,000

Member State	Date of Admission	Scale of Assessments (per cent)	Population (est.)
Malta	1 December 1964	0.01	383,000
Mauritania	27 October 1961	0.01	1,888,000
Mauritius	24 April 1968	0.01	1,020,000
Mexico	7 November 1945	0.89	78,524,000
Mongolia	27 October 1961	0.01	1,915,000
Morocco	12 November 1956	0.05	21,941,000
Mozambique	16 September 1975	0.01	13,961,000
Nepal	14 December 1955	0.01	16,625,000
Netherlands	10 December 1945	1.74	14,484,000
New Zealand	24 October 1945	0.24	3,291,000
Nicaragua	24 October 1945	0.01	3,272,000
Niger	20 September 1960	0.01	6,115,000
Nigeria	7 October 1960	0.19	95,198,000
Norway	27 November 1945	0.54	4,153,000
Oman	7 October 1971	0.02	2,000,000
Pakistan	30 September 1947	0.06	99,163,000
Panama	13 November 1945	0.02	2,227,000
Papua New Guinea	10 October 1975	0.01	3,329,000
Paraguay	24 October 1945	0.02	3,681,000
Peru	31 October 1945	0.07	19,698,000
Philippines	24 October 1945	0.10	54,378,000
Poland	24 October 1945	0.64	37,528,000
Portugal	14 December 1955	0.18	10,229,000
Qatar	21 September 1971	0.04	315,000
Romania	14 December 1955	0.19	23,017,000
Rwanda	18 September 1962	0.01	6,274,000
Saint Kitts and Nevis	23 September 1983	0.01	46,000
Saint Lucia	18 September 1979	0.01	130,000
Saint Vincent and the Grenadines	16 September 1980	0.01	104,000
Samoa	15 December 1976	0.01	163,000
Sao Tome and Principe	16 September 1975	0.01	108,000
Saudi Arabia	24 October 1945	0.97	11,542,000
Senegal	28 September 1960	0.01	6,444,000
Seychelles	21 September 1976	0.01	66,000
Sierra Leone	27 September 1961	0.01	3,516,000
Singapore[f]	21 September 1965	0.10	2,586,000
Solomon Islands	19 September 1978	0.01	270,000
Somalia	20 September 1960	0.01	4,653,000
South Africa	7 November 1945	0.44	32,392,000
Spain	14 December 1955	2.03	38,818,000
Sri Lanka	14 December 1955	0.01	15,837,000
Sudan	12 November 1956	0.01	21,550,000
Suriname	4 December 1975	0.01	375,000
Swaziland	24 September 1968	0.01	647,000
Sweden	19 November 1946	1.25	8,374,000
Syrian Arab Republic	24 October 1945	0.04	10,267,000
Thailand	16 December 1946	0.09	51,301,000

170

Member State	Date of Admission	Scale of Assessments (per cent)	Population (est.)
Togo	20 September 1960	0.01	2,960,000
Trinidad and Tobago	18 September 1962	0.04	1,185,000
Tunisia	12 November 1956	0.03	7,261,000
Turkey	24 October 1945	0.34	49,272,000
Uganda	25 October 1962	0.01	15,477,000
Ukrainian Soviet Socialist Republic	24 October 1945	1.28	50,800,000[g]
Union of Soviet Socialist Republics	24 October 1945	10.20	280,100,000
United Arab Emirates	9 December 1971	0.18	1,327,000
United Kingdom of Great Britain and Northern Ireland	24 October 1945	4.86	56,618,000
United Republic of Tanzania[h]	14 December 1961	0.01	21,733,000
United States of America	24 October 1945	25.00	239,283,000
Uruguay	18 December 1945	0.04	2,931,000
Vanuatu	15 September 1981	0.01	142,000
Venezuela	15 November 1945	0.60	17,317,000
Viet Nam	20 September 1977	0.01	59,713,000
Yemen	30 September 1947	0.01	9,274,000
Yugoslavia	24 October 1945	0.46	23,236,000
Zaire	20 September 1960	0.01	30,363,000
Zambia	1 December 1964	0.01	6,666,000
Zimbabwe	25 August 1980	0.02	8,379,000

[a]Formerly Dahomey.

[b]Formerly the Upper Volta.

[c]By resolution 2758 (XXVI) of 25 October 1971, the General Assembly decided "to restore all its rights to the People's Republic of China and to recognize the representatives of its Government as the only legitimate representatives of China to the United Nations, and to expel forthwith the representatives of Chiang Kai-shek from the place they unlawfully occupy at the United Nations and in all the organizations related to it".

[d]Formerly Cambodia.

[e]Egypt and Syria were original Members of the United Nations from 24 October 1945. Following a plebiscite on 21 January 1958, the United Arab Republic was established by a union of Egypt and Syria and continued as a single Member. On 13 October 1961, Syria resumed its status as an independent State and simultaneously its United Nations membership. On 2 September 1971, the United Arab Republic changed its name to Arab Republic of Egypt.

[f]The Federation of Malaya joined the United Nations on 17 September 1957. On 16 September 1963, its name was changed to Malaysia, following the admission to the new federation of Singapore, Sabah (North Borneo) and Sarawak. Singapore became an independent State on 9 August 1965 and a United Nations Member on 21 September 1965.

[g]Includes population of Byelorussian SSR and Ukrainian SSR.

[h]Tanganyika was a United Nations Member from 14 December 1961 and Zanzibar was a Member from 16 December 1963. Following the ratification on 26 April 1964 of Articles of Union between Tanganyika and Zanzibar, the United Republic of Tanganyika and Zanzibar continued as a single Member, changing its name to the United Republic of Tanzania on 1 November 1964.

UNITED NATIONS INFORMATION CENTRES AND SERVICES

Centres and Services in Africa

ACCRA • United Nations Information Centre, Gamel Abdul Nassar/Liberia Roads (Post Office Box 2339), Accra, Ghana
▶ *Services to:* Ghana, Sierra Leone

ADDIS ABABA • United Nations Information Service, Economic Commission for Africa, Africa Hall (Post Office Box 3001), Addis Ababa, Ethiopia
▶ *Services to:* Ethiopia

ALGIERS • United Nations Information Centre, 19, avenue Chahid el-Ouali, Mustapha Sayed (Boîte postale 823), Algiers, Algeria
▶ *Services to:* Algeria

ANTANANARIVO • United Nations Information Centre, 22, rue Rainitovo, Antsahavola (Boîte Postale 1348), Antananarivo, Madagascar
▶ *Services to:* Madagascar

BRAZZAVILLE • United Nations Information Centre, avenue Pointe-Hollandaise, Quartier M'Pila (Boîte postale 465), Brazzaville, Congo
▶ *Services to:* Congo

BUJUMBURA • United Nations Information Centre, avenue de la Poste 7, place de l'Indépendance (Boîte postale 2160), Bujumbura, Burundi
▶ *Services to:* Burundi

CAIRO • United Nations Information Centre, 1 Osiris Street, Tagher Building (Garden City) (Boîte postale 262), Cairo, Egypt
▶ *Services to:* Egypt, Saudi Arabia, Yemen

DAKAR • United Nations Information Centre, 9, allées Robert Delmas (Boîte postale 154), Dakar, Senegal
▶ *Services to:* Cape Verde, Côte d'Ivoire, Gambia, Guinea, Guinea-Bissau, Mauritania, Senegal

DAR ES SALAAM • United Nations Information Centre, Samora Machel Avenue, Matasalamat Building, 1st Floor (Post Office Box 9224), Dar es Salaam, United Republic of Tanzania
▶ *Services to:* United Republic of Tanzania

HARARE • United Nations Information Centre, Dolphin House, 123 Moffat Street/Union Avenue (Post Office Box 4408), Harare, Zimbabwe
▶ *Services to:* Zimbabwe

KHARTOUM • United Nations Information Centre, Gasser Avenue, Street No. 15, Block 3, House 3, Khartoum East, Khartoum, Sudan
▶ *Services to:* Somalia, Sudan

KINSHASA • United Nations Information Centre, Bâtiment Deuxième République, boulevard du 30 juin (Boîte postale 7248), Kinshasa, Zaire
▶ *Services to:* Zaire

LAGOS • United Nations Information Centre, 17 Kingsway Road, Ikoyi (Post Office Box 1068), Lagos, Nigeria
▶ *Services to:* Nigeria

LOME • United Nations Information Centre, 107 boulevard du 13 janvier (Boîte postale 911), Lomé, Togo
▶ *Services to:* Benin, Togo

LUSAKA • United Nations Information Centre, Post Office Box 32905, Lusaka, Zambia
▶ *Services to:* Botswana, Malawi, Swaziland, Zambia

MASERU • United Nations Information Centre, Corner Kingsway and Hilton Roads, Opposite Sanlam Centre (Post Office Box 301), Maseru 100, Lesotho
  ‣ *Services to:* Lesotho

MONROVIA • United Nations Information Centre, LBDI Building, Tubman Boulevard (Post Office Box 274), Monrovia, Liberia
  ‣ *Services to:* Liberia

NAIROBI • United Nations Information Centre, United Nations Office, Gigiri (Post Office Box 34135), Nairobi, Kenya
  ‣ *Services to:* Kenya, Seychelles, Uganda

OUAGADOUGOU • United Nations Information Centre, 218, rue de la Gare, Secteur n$^{o.}$ 3 (Boîte postale 135), Ouagadougou, Burkina Faso
  ‣ *Services to:* Burkina Faso, Chad, Mali, Niger

RABAT • United Nations Information Centre, angle Charia Moulay Ibnouzaid et Zankat Roundanat ("Casier ONU"), Rabat-Chellah, Morocco
  ‣ *Services to:* Morocco

TRIPOLI • United Nations Information Centre, Muzaffar Al Aftas Street, Hay El-Andolous (Post Office Box 286), Tripoli, Libyan Arab Jamahiriya
  ‣ *Services to:* Libyan Arab Jamahiriya

TUNIS • United Nations Information Centre, 61 boulevard Bab-Benat (Boîte postale 863), Tunis, Tunisia
  ‣ *Services to:* Tunisia

YAOUNDE • United Nations Information Centre, Immeuble Kamden, rue Joseph Clère (Boîte postale 836), Yaoundé, Cameroon
  ‣ *Services to:* Cameroon, Central African Republic, Gabon

Centres and Services in the Americas

ASUNCION • United Nations Information Centre, Casilla de Correo 1107, Asunción, Paraguay
  ‣ *Services to:* Paraguay

BOGOTA • United Nations Information Centre, Calle 72, No. 12-65, piso 2 (Apartado Aéreo 058964), Bogotá 2, Colombia
  ‣ *Services to:* Colombia, Ecuador, Venezuela

BUENOS AIRES • United Nations Information Centre, Junín 1940, 1er piso, 1113 Buenos Aires, Argentina
  ‣ *Services to:* Argentina, Uruguay

LA PAZ • United Nations Information Centre, Edificio Naciones Unidas, Plaza Isabel La Católica, Ex-Clínica Santa Isabel, Planta Baja (Apartado Postal 686), La Paz, Bolivia
  ‣ *Services to:* Bolivia

LIMA • United Nations Information Centre, Mariscal Blas Cerdeña 450, San Isidro (Apartado Postal 14-0199), Lima, Peru
  ‣ *Services to:* Peru

MANAGUA • United Nations Information Centre, Bolonia, de Plaza España, 2 cuadras abajo (Apartado Postal 3260), Managua, Nicaragua
  ‣ *Services to:* Nicaragua

MEXICO CITY • United Nations Information Centre, Presidente Mazaryk 29, 7° piso, México 11570, D.F., México
  ‣ *Services to:* Cuba, Dominican Republic, Mexico

PANAMA CITY • United Nations Information Centre, Urbanización Obarrio, Calle 54 y Avenida Tercera Sur, Edificio N$^{o.}$ 17 (Apartado Postal 6-9083 El Dorado), Panama City, Panamá
  ‣ *Services to:* Panama

PORT OF SPAIN ● United Nations Information Centre, 15 Keate Street (Post Office Box 130), Port of Spain, Trinidad
  ▶ *Services to:* Antigua and Barbuda, Bahamas, Barbados, Belize, Dominica, Grenada, Guyana, Jamaica, Netherlands Antilles, Saint Kitts and Nevis, Saint Lucia, Saint Vincent and the Grenadines, Suriname, Trinidad and Tobago

RIO DE JANEIRO ● United Nations Information Centre, Palacio Itamaraty, Avenida Marechal Floriano 196, Rio de Janeiro, RJ Brazil
  ▶ *Services to:* Brazil

SAN SALVADOR ● United Nations Information Centre, Edificio Escalón, 2° piso, Paseo General Escalón y 87 Avenida Norte, Colonia Escalón (Apartado Postal 2157), San Salvador, El Salvador
  ▶ *Services to:* El Salvador

SANTIAGO ● United Nations Information Service, Economic Commission for Latin America and the Caribbean, Edificio Naciones Unidas, Avenida Dag Hammarskjöld (Casilla 179-D), Santiago, Chile
  ▶ *Services to:* Chile

WASHINGTON ● United Nations Information Centre, 1889 F Street, N.W., Washington, D.C. 20006, United States
  ▶ *Services to:* United States

Centres and Services in Asia and Oceania

ANKARA ● United Nations Information Centre, 197 Atatürk Bulvari (P.K. 407), Ankara, Turkey
  ▶ *Services to:* Turkey

BAGHDAD ● United Nations Information Service, Economic and Social Commission for Western Asia, Amiriya, Airport Street (Post Office Box 27), Baghdad, Iraq
  ▶ *Services to:* Iraq

BANGKOK ● United Nations Information Service, Economic and Social Commission for Asia and the Pacific, United Nations Building, Rajdamnern Avenue, Bangkok 10200, Thailand
  ▶ *Services to:* Democratic Kampuchea, Lao People's Democratic Republic, Malaysia, Singapore, Thailand, Viet Nam

BEIRUT ● United Nations Information Centre, Apartment No. 1, Fakhoury Building, Montée Bain Militaire, Ardati Street (Post Office Box 4656), Beirut, Lebanon
  ▶ *Services to:* Jordan, Kuwait, Lebanon, Syrian Arab Republic

COLOMBO ● United Nations Information Centre, 202-204 Bauddhaloka Mawatha (Post Office Box 1505), Colombo 7, Sri Lanka
  ▶ *Services to:* Sri Lanka

DHAKA ● United Nations Information Centre, House 12, Road 6, Dhanmandi (General Post Office Box 3658, Dhaka 100), Dhaka 1205, Bangladesh
  ▶ *Services to:* Bangladesh

ISLAMABAD ● United Nations Information Centre, House No. 26, 88th Street, Ramna 16/3 (Post Office Box 1107), Islamabad, Pakistan
  ▶ *Services to:* Pakistan

JAKARTA ● United Nations Information Centre, Gedung Dewan Pers, 5th Floor, 32-34 Jalan Kebon Sirih, Jakarta, Indonesia
  ▶ *Services to:* Indonesia

KABUL ● United Nations Information Centre, Shah Mahmoud Ghazi Watt (Post Office Box 5), Kabul, Afghanistan
  ▶ *Services to:* Afghanistan

KATHMANDU ● United Nations Information Centre, Pulchowk, Patan (Post Office Box 107), Kathmandu, Nepal
  ▶ *Services to:* Nepal

MANAMA ● United Nations Information Centre, King Faisal Road, Gufool (Post Office Box 26004), Manama, Bahrain
  ‣ *Services to:* Bahrain, Qatar, United Arab Emirates

MANILA ● United Nations Information Centre, Ground Floor, NEDA Building, 106 Amorsolo Street, Legaspi Village, Makati (Post Office Box 7285 (ADC), MIA Road, Pasay City), Metro Manila, Philippines
  ‣ *Services to:* Papua New Guinea, Philippines, Solomon Islands

NEW DELHI ● United Nations Information Centre, 55 Lodi Estate, New Delhi 110 003, India
  ‣ *Services to:* Bhutan, India

RANGOON ● United Nations Information Centre, 28A, Manawhari Road (Post Office Box 230), Rangoon, Burma
  ‣ *Services to:* Burma

SYDNEY ● United Nations Information Centre, National Mutual Centre, 44 Market Street, 16th Floor (Post Office Box 4045), Sydney, N.S.W. 2001, Australia
  ‣ *Services to:* Australia, Fiji, Kiribati, Nauru, New Zealand, Samoa, Tonga, Tuvalu, Vanuatu

TEHERAN ● United Nations Information Centre, Avenue Gandhi, 43 Street No. 3 (Post Office Box 1555), Teheran, Iran
  ‣ *Services to:* Iran

TOKYO ● United Nations Information Centre, Shin Aoyama Building Nishika, 22nd Floor, 1-1 Minami Aoyama 1-chome, Minato-ku, Tokyo 107, Japan
  ‣ *Services to:* Japan, Trust Territory of the Pacific Islands

Centres and Services in Europe

ATHENS ● United Nations Information Centre, 36 Amalia Avenue, GR-105, 58 Athens, Greece
  ‣ *Services to:* Cyprus, Greece, Israel

BELGRADE ● United Nations Information Centre, Svetozara Markovica 58 (Post Office Box 157), Belgrade, Yugoslavia YU-11001
  ‣ *Services to:* Albania, Yugoslavia

BRUSSELS ● United Nations Information Centre and Liaison Office, 108 rue d'Arlon, 1040 Brussels, Belgium
  ‣ *Services to:* Belgium, Luxembourg, Netherlands

BUCHAREST ● United Nations Information Centre, 16 Aurel Vlaicu Street (Post Office Box 1-701), Bucharest, Romania
  ‣ *Services to:* Romania

COPENHAGEN ● United Nations Information Centre, 37 H. C. Andersen Boulevard, DK-1553 Copenhagen V, Denmark
  ‣ *Services to:* Denmark, Finland, Iceland, Norway, Sweden

GENEVA ● United Nations Information Service, United Nations Office at Geneva, Palais des Nations, 1211 Geneva 10, Switzerland
  ‣ *Services to:* Bulgaria, Hungary, Poland, Switzerland

LISBON ● United Nations Information Centre, Rua Latino Coelho No. 1, Edificio Aviz, Bloco A1-10°, 1000 Lisbon, Portugal
  ‣ *Services to:* Portugal

LONDON ● United Nations Information Centre, Ship House, 20 Buckingham Gate, London SW1E 6LB, England
  ‣ *Services to:* Ireland, United Kingdom

MADRID ● United Nations Information Centre, Avenida General Perón, 32-1° (Post Office Box 3.400, 28080), 28020 Madrid, Spain
  ‣ *Services to:* Spain

MOSCOW • United Nations Information Centre, 4/16 Ulitsa Lunacharskogo, Moscow 121002, USSR
  ▸ *Services to:* Byelorussian SSR, Ukrainian SSR, USSR

PARIS • United Nations Information Centre, 1 rue Miollis, 75732, Paris Cedex 15, France
  ▸ *Services to:* France

PRAGUE • United Nations Information Centre, Panska 5, 11000 Prague 1, Czechoslovakia
  ▸ *Services to:* Czechoslovakia, German Democratic Republic

ROME • United Nations Information Centre, Palazzetto Venezia, Piazza San Marco 50, Rome, Italy
  ▸ *Services to:* Holy See, Italy, Malta

VIENNA • United Nations Information Service, United Nations Office at Vienna, Vienna International Centre, Wagramer Strasse 5 (Post Office Box 500, A-1400) A-1220 Vienna, Austria
  ▸ *Services to:* Austria, Federal Republic of Germany

UNITED NATIONS SPECIAL OBSERVANCES

International Decades and Years

1978-1988	Transport and Communications Decade in Africa
1980s	Industrial Development Decade for Africa
1980s	Second Disarmament Decade
1981-1990	International Drinking Water Supply and Sanitation Decade
1981-1990	Third United Nations Development Decade
1983-1992	United Nations Decade of Disabled Persons
1983-1993	Second Decade to Combat Racism and Racial Discrimination
1985-1994	Transport and Communications Decade for Asia and the Pacific
1987	International Year of Shelter for the Homeless
1988-1997	World Decade for Cultural Development

Annual Days and Weeks

21 March	International Day for the Elimination of Racial Discrimination
Beginning 21 March	Week of Solidarity with the Peoples Struggling against Racism and Racial Discrimination
Beginning 25 May	Week of Solidarity with the Peoples of Namibia and All Other Colonial Territories, as well as those in South Africa, Fighting for Freedom, Independence and Human Rights
4 June	International Day of Innocent Children Victims of Aggression
5 June	World Environment Day
16 June	International Day of Solidarity with the Struggling People of South Africa
9 August	International Day of Solidarity with the Struggle of Women in South Africa and Namibia
26 August	Namibia Day
Third Tuesday of September	International Day of Peace
First Monday of October	World Habitat Day
11 October	Day of Solidarity with South African Political Prisoners
16 October	World Food Day
24 October	United Nations Day
24-30 October	Disarmament Week
Week of 27 October	Week of Solidarity with the People of Namibia and Their Liberation Movement, SWAPO
29 November	International Day of Solidarity with the Palestinian People
5 December	International Volunteer Day for Economic and Social Development
10 December	Human Rights Day

Other International Days

Other international days observed throughout the United Nations system include:

International Women's Day (8 March), World Maritime Day (during the last week in September), World Meteorological Day (23 March), World Health Day (7 April), World Telecommunication Day (17 May), International Literacy Day (8 September), Universal Children's Day (varies; traditionally first Monday of October), World Post Day (9 October) and World Development Information Day (24 October).

177

FOR FURTHER READING*

The Blue Helmets, a review of United Nations peace-keeping (350 pages) (DPI/850; Sales No. E.85.I.18, paper, $8.95)

Charter of the United Nations and Statute of the International Court of Justice (87 pages) (OPI/511; $1.00)

Everyman's United Nations (8th edition, 1945-1965, 634 pages) (Sales No. E.67.I.2, cloth, $10.00)

Everyone's United Nations
(9th edition, 1966-1978, 477 pages) (DPI/625; Sales No. E.79.I.5: cloth, $12.50; paper, $7.95)
(10th edition, 1978-1985, 484 pages) (DPI/855; Sales No. E.85.I.24: cloth, $14.95; paper, $9.95)
   Note: Special price for 8th and 9th editions, clothbound: $20.00.

Image & Reality, Questions and answers about United Nations management, finance and people (40 pages) (DPI/872; $1.25)

The International Bill of Human Rights (44 pages) (DPI/797; $2.00)

The International Court of Justice (9th edition, 45 pages) (DPI/780; Sales No. 83.I.20, $2.00)

International Development Strategy for the Third United Nations Development Decade (27 pages) (DPI/689; $2.00)

Objective: Justice (issued twice a year) (annual subscription, $10.00; single issue, $5.00)

A Quiet Revolution: The United Nations Convention on the Law of the Sea (61 pages) (DPI/786; Sales No. E.83.V.7, $5.00)

Pope John Paul II at the United Nations (64 pages, illustrated) (DPI/645; Sales No. E.80.I.8: cloth, $9.50; paper, $4.95)

UN Chronicle (4 issues a year, illustrated) (annual subscription, $14.00)

The United Nations and Decolonization (48 pages, illustrated) (DPI/678; 2 dollars)

The United Nations and Drug Abuse Control (101 pages) (DPI/906; Sales No. E.87.I.8, $5.00)

The United Nations and Human Rights (267 pages) (DPI/808; Sales No. E.84.I.6, $5.00)

The United Nations Treaties on Outer Space (37 pages) (DPI/810; Sales No. E.84.I.10, $2.00)

The Universal Declaration of Human Rights (15 pages) (DPI/876, 35 cents)

Yearbook of the United Nations (issued annually) (Vol. 37, 1983, 1,431 pages) (Sales No. E.86.I.1; $85.00)

Your United Nations: (The Official Guidebook) (96 pages, illustrated) (Sales No. E.82.I.10: cloth, $9.95; paper, $5.95)

* Selected list of publications issued by the United Nations Department of Public Information. For a complete list of United Nations publications in print, write to:

United Nations Publications
Sales Section
Room DC2-0853
New York, N.Y. 10017
United States of America

or

United Nations Publications
Sales Section
Palais des Nations
1211 Geneva, Switzerland

DPI/915—14000—October 1987—70M